HEDINGHAM HARVEST

GEOFFREY ROBINSON

HEDINGHAM HARVEST

Victorian family life
in rural England

CONSTABLE
LONDON

First published in Great Britain 1977
by Constable and Company Ltd
3 The Lanchesters, 162 Fulham Palace Road
London W6 9ER
Paperback edition 1996
Copyright © 1977 Geoffrey Robinson
ISBN 0 09 476600 2
Printed in Great Britain by
St Edmundsbury Press Ltd,
Bury St Edmunds, Suffolk

A CIP catalogue record for this book
is available from the British Library

Preface

Since the age of twelve I have been an inveterate recorder of my relatives' accounts of life in Lincolnshire. The older the relative the more urgent, it seemed to me, was the need to squeeze him dry of his recollections before the grave silenced him. Fortunately, my grandparents lived to be very old, their memories were good, and they loved to recall the past. I had fourteen garrulous aunts and uncles, and a mother who talked less but wrote more. Thus, one way or another, I can give a fairly detailed account of rural life in Lincolnshire towards the end of the nineteenth century, and if it seems surprisingly un-Victorian, that is how it has been described to me by people who lived then. They were my maternal relatives because my father's family did not come from Lincolnshire but from Glinton, a village a few miles over the border into Northamptonshire.

Three family trees are shown at the end of the book to clarify the relationship between the numerous people mentioned in it. Of my grandparents' eight children, my Uncle Henry will be the central figure notwith-standing that my mother was, in her way, almost as interesting a character; but she saw Lincolnshire with the eyes of an impressionist painter. Her vision was blurred by emotion and sensibility. Shapes for her were imprecise, and I prefer the clear, cool, unsentimental gaze of her brother Henry, who was not only the most robust but the most intelligent of the family, the most musical, and the most hag-ridden by ambition and sensuality. Nevertheless, my mother provided much of the material for this book, and it is dedicated to her. The story is set in Hedingham and there is, of course, no such village in Lincolnshire. Those who know the district will recognize similarities with Waddingham, near Brigg, but the resemblance is by no means complete. Therefore a reader should not conclude that Waddingham had a rector who slept with his maids, nor a miller's wife who slept with my grandfather, because I only warrant that there was such a rector, and such a miller's wife, in the locality.

Lincolnshire is thought to be flat, but it is not. Hedingham is on an escarpment which at Kirton Lindsey, a few miles away, drops sharply into the Trent valley. The tall ridge of the Wolds shelters Hedingham on the east, and Lincoln itself stands on as steep a hill as anyone could wish not to climb. It is the fens in the south, the hideous bulb-fields and the marvellous skies, that have given Lincolnshire its reputation. This book has nothing to do with those parts of the County rightly called Holland; salvaged from swamps, and as dull as the ditchwater from which they came. I write about northern Lincolnshire, although parts of it are now afflicted with the name of 'Humberside'. Perhaps Hedingham is not today in Lincolnshire at all—I have not been able to bring myself to inquire. It certainly used to be.

Durham, 1977   G.R.

Active though he was with a succession of servant girls and neighbours' wives, my grandfather did not neglect to shake almost nightly with his reluctant wife the kaleidoscope of family genes. It settled for my Uncle Henry into a design so brightly coloured and so exceptional within the family that the possibility of an advantageous maternal adultery might have been suspected if my grandmother's disinterest in sex had not made such a supposition entirely implausible. An explanation of why Henry was, as some said, 'born beneath him' must be hidden within the undeciphered rules of the genetic lottery. My grandmother was well aware of the uncertainty of the prizes, and after each of her deliveries the first question to Aunt Hiles, the family midwife, was not, 'Is it a boy?' She was more concerned to ask, 'Has it all its fingers and toes?' Henry had a full complement of both, and a great deal more besides, as the village schoolmaster was soon to discover.

All the eight children, five boys and three girls, were born between 1879 and 1892 in a square house of Lincolnshire brick, looking out on to the Green of Hedingham, a sprawling, untidy, village seventeen miles north of Lincoln, off Ermine Street, the old Roman road to Brigg. Their father, Edward Maitland Fisher, was the village blacksmith and his maternal grandfather, Robert Maitland, was the Fishers' claim to gentility. Every family has its links with the gentry on the right or wrong side of the blanket, links real or supposed ; and Robert Maitland was the ancestor who gave us that difference from the others which could have no explanation but that he was of the Scottish peerage. The great advantage of attaching the myth of nobility to Robert Maitland was that nothing was known of him, except for a family tradition of his having come down from the north to be the Hedingham farrier. His son, Richard Maitland, another blacksmith, adopted my grandfather and gave him his indentures of apprenticeship in the trade, so it may strain credulity to add that the Fishers themselves had for generations been blacksmiths near Nottingham, and that my grandfather married the daughter of another blacksmith, Thomas Millson of Redbourne. Nevertheless it is true ; and if my grandfather had ever achieved, or purchased, a coat of arms, he could have done nothing but fill every quarter of it with hammers, anvils, pincers and bellows.

The blacksmith's shop in Hedingham lay alongside the house. Its doors stood open all day with two red fires glowing in the gloom inside, ready to be blown into white incandescence by foot-bellows when iron was to be softened for shaping. My grandfather and the journeyman, Steeper Dickson, worked together and the sound of their hammers rang out into the village, a long percussion when the hammer struck the white-hot iron, then two short ones on the anvil to cool the hammer for its next blow. The huge Lincolnshire carthorses stood tethered near the doors for their new shoes to be clapped on almost red hot, with a puff of smoke from the seared hoof, and the acrid smell drifting over the Green. Farm carts stood, shafts uptilted, in the blacksmith's yard for their wheels to be shod with iron hoops, shaped hot on quadrant templates that were hung, when not in use, on the outside walls of the forge as the

8

symbol of the trade carried on inside it. When rounded to the correct size the rims were reheated to expand them for fitting, then as they cooled they shrank and bit their own smoking groove into the circumference of the wooden wheels.

Horses' hooves and cartwheels provided the basic living for the blacksmith, though he would turn his hand to a great variety of iron working. One of my grandfather's books of account has survived and it demonstrates the wide range of his trade and how little he earned by practising it. I set out some typical entries :

	£	s.	d.
4 shoes		2	0
Horse roughed		1	0
3 pigs' ringing			6
Scythe shaft		1	6
Window rod lengthened			2
Shoe horn			4
Gig shaft repaired			8
6 Harrow teeth put in			3
Wheel bushing for dray		1	6
Saucepan handle put on			2
Kettle spout put in			4
2 bolts for engine		1	6
Gate sneck repaired			6
2 plates for boot heels			6
Turnip chopper and shaft		2	0
Hoop for churn			8
1 candlestick			4
Lock repaired			3
2½ ft of chain for gear			9
Carriage step repaired			4
New iron bedstead	1	10	0
Grindstone handle and axe		2	6
Boy assisting organ mender		2	8
Organ bellows handle		5	0
Coffee mill repaired			6

	£	s.	d.
Perambulator repaired			3
Cake breaker repaired		2	0
2 bacon hooks			8

The account book shows that the bills delivered for the work of a blacksmith, a journeyman and an apprentice amounted in total to about two hundred and fifty pounds a year, which is consistent with the charge of four shillings when grandfather or his journeyman was hired to work by the day. Thus, in the rural market when a farm labourer was paid thirty pounds a year, a blacksmith could earn about one hundred and twenty, while the stipend of the Bishop of Lincoln was four thousand five hundred. The level of the market for a farrier was determined by the tramp black-smiths on the Great North Road who were ready to move into any locality where the demand for a blacksmith's ser-vices sufficiently exceeded the supply for one of them to scratch a non-itinerant living there. The level of the market for a farm labourer was fixed by the need to keep him alive and able to do a long day's work ; and the market for bishops was fixed, I suppose, by God.

My Uncle Henry began life in 1883 with half the chromosomes of a father who, through a long agricultural depression, forced his way from village blacksmith to strug-gling tenant farmer and then, with the windfall of the Great War, to become the owner of five hundred acres of rather poor land. His maternal inheritance was less intelligence, but an equal fortitude—or his mother could not have sur-vived a quick succession of pregnancies and marriage to a hot-tempered, domineering, mean, and exceedingly adul-terous husband. That she gave birth to only eight children was due to her not marrying until she was thirty. Otherwise she would have followed the common pattern of having many more. Even if most village wives would have bartered fewer pregnancies for less sexual intercourse, there were few husbands of that inclination, and my grandfather was not one of them. In Protestant rural Lincolnshire, coitus interruptus was the usual method of birth control, so unless a wife happened to be infertile or had married late or had died young, usually in childbirth, she would have a very large number of children. If my more remote forebears were any guide, fourteen or more was common, and the rudimentary medical services allowed natural selection to work freely upon them. Deaths in infancy were frequent and those who survived the childhood hazards of measles, croup, whooping-cough, scarlet fever, smallpox, chicken pox, rheumatic fever, diphtheria and meningitis, still had to face the scythe of tuberculosis that cut swathes through the youth of many village families. However, all my grandmother's children survived the many infections that nature tossed their way to test their fitness to breed; and they did it despite the attentions of Doctor Rainbird, with his bottle of black leeches, who was rather an aid to natural selection than a hindrance. He was a large, bluff, cheerful man, and he treated all the many ills for which he knew no other remedy in the same way. He lifted his leeches from the bottle with a pair of forceps and laid them on his patients' temples with little comforting inarticulate murmurs, like a priest hurrying through the Mass. Once there, nothing could detach them till they had gorged themselves with blood. Then they fell off, replete, and were carried away again for their next meal.

Yet whatever his professional shortcomings, Doctor Rainbird had charm and my mother, at the age of seventeen, fell subject to it while he was supposed to be treating her for diphtheria. She recovered from the illness, but not from her physician; and my brother owes his initials P.H.R. to the after-effects of her medical treatment, which included gifts of scent and flowers, and visits to the doctor's lovely house, where peacocks strutted on the lawns. When nearly eighty, my mother could write: 'Percival Horace Rainbird, my first love, is never forgotten—let me bury my face in lilacs, or see long-stemmed single rosebuds, or baby peacocks, or put eau-de-Cologne on a handkerchief, or write P.H.R. to my younger son.'

By the time Henry was born, his father was already farming twelve acres of Glebe land while running the blacksmith's shop, but for the next eleven years he was unable, through shortage of capital, to increase the size of his smallholding. Throughout the most impressionable years of Henry's life he was to all intents and purposes the son of a blacksmith, but whereas many intelligent sons of blacksmiths became engineers and founded ironworks, like Robert Robey and John Cooke, Henry did not derive from his environment the slightest interest in things mechanical. Nor did any of his brothers, and the reason may be that far from identifying with their father, they thoroughly disliked him. And so did his sisters. My mother always regarded herself as bound to obey the commandment to honour her father, but she could never even pretend to love him. He had frightened her too often when she was young. He was tall and thin, with brown hair and a ginger moustache and of a 'commanding appearance'. All his children testified to his terrifying rages, which were all the more fearsome for their lack of violence. He had cold blue eyes that in anger did not light up and blaze. They went even colder till they were so bleak and drained of humanity that a child was cut off and exiled from the possibility even of understanding. Punishment lacked human warmth too. Grandfather seldom struck his children in anger upon discovering an offence. He practised instead the studied cruelty of saying that he would give the offender a 'threshing' the next day, and he did. For the boy it was with a stick and for a girl it was with his hand.

Apart from beating his sons, and teaching them to box so that they could beat others, and apart from making them work before and after school in his fields, grandfather was unconcerned with them. It never occurred to him that children needed to be amused or entertained. According to my mother, 'he almost seemed to dislike us.' He never embraced or caressed his children, although he required his daughters to kiss him goodnight before they went to bed, and he kissed them on Christmas morning underneath the 'mistletoe bough', when his red moustache tickled. Above all, he was mean. He never gave a birthday present and my mother could not remember ever having had so much as a halfpenny from him, nor a sweet. Yet I can record that not one of his sons and daughters ever had a nervous breakdown, took sedatives, smoked heavily or drank to excess. None showed as an adult any sign of neurosis that I could discern and certainly none needed treatment in a mental hospital or by a psychiatrist. So though my grandfather was an unloved parent he reared eight very stable children, and for those of them who could benefit, like Henry, he happened also to be stimulating.

Amongst the master craftsmen of the village, my grandfather and his cousin Charlie Rudkin were the intellectuals. Uncle Charlie was the more clever of the two and since he profoundly influenced the young Henry I will write more of him later, but grandfather himself was no yokel. He was sharply intelligent, scathing and intolerant. Any slow-witted though kindly man he dismissed as a 'ninny-nonny'. For his own education he read Pope, and considered 'An Essay on Man' to be the true philosophy. He was particularly fond of Shakespeare and liked Tennyson and Dickens. He read Charles Kingsley's *Hypatia* over and over again. For himself he took *Farm, Field and Fireside* and the *Cornhill Magazine*, and the children had *Cassell's Home Educator*, *Cassell's Magazine*, *Pearson's Magazine*, and the *Boy's Own Paper*. He encouraged them to think for themselves and opened their minds to the issues of the day. Conversation at meals was on serious and important questions. There was little small talk because he had neither the inclination nor the slightest talent for it ; but he so loved to argue on general issues that he couldn't resist engaging even his family, whose opinions he despised, in discussions on religion and on political questions such as free trade or protection, the growth of trades unions and home rule for Ireland. In politics he was a Liberal and in religion he was a free thinker, having lapsed from Wesleyanism when he outgrew his youthful taste for singing bass in the chapel choir. From the turgid block harmonies of Moody and Sankey, the revivalist hymn book, he moved to the comparative sophistication of glee singing and thereby lost his only temperamental link with religious experience.

If the blacksmith provided his children with a father to fear and admire, his wife provided them with a mother to love and respect. She was quiet, slim and handsome, but her gentle exterior overlay a strength of will more powerful than her husband's. She deferred to him only until he overstepped her limits of subjection. Then, after announcing that she was 'sick and surfeited' she would attack, and it was grandfather who retreated from the battlefield. Her ultimate power over him was absolute because he loved her more than she loved him, and both knew it. An imbalance of affection must be endemic in marriage, though often hidden by disguises. The two Fishers concealed the preponderance of the husband's love under his reluctance to reveal any feelings at all, except anger and frustration, and under her willingness to appear to do, most of the time, what the marriage service demanded. But grandfather knew that Bessie Millson had married him only for his name. Another Edward Fisher had been the object of the overwhelming and disappointed love of her adolescence. Grandmother had been in service in Lincoln with a maiden lady whose nephew, Edward Fisher, was a frequent visitor. Bessie and he fell in love, and his scandalized parents removed him to Australia. The son of the Town Clerk of Lincoln might sleep with a housemaid, but not love her. My grandmother was then eighteen and it was not until twelve years later that she married another man, but with the same name. My Aunt Matilda said, with her usual contempt for the passions, that by then she had 'got over that silly spasm', but my grandfather knew better. He was well aware that he lived in the shadow of that bright youth, not merely as his substitute—for many suffer that—but as his namesake. The wound to his self-esteem never quite healed and my grandmother never entirely forgave the upper-middle classes for having rejected her. However, although she suffered the early mortification of not being good enough for the son of a solicitor, she later enjoyed the irony, if not the satisfaction, of becoming the mother of one. I must, however, make clear that her son Henry was really a foundling, laid on the doorstep of the profession. He was not of the bloodstock, those middle ranks of the middle public schools, that gave provincial attorneys their distinctive flavour of having none. Henry was a very atypical, even eccentric, solicitor, and his formal education began and ended in his native village.

Hedingham School was on the far side of the Green, across from the blacksmith's house and all the Fisher children, John, James, Henry, Mary, Robert, Matilda, George, and Fanny, went there. They started at the age of four and left on their thirteenth birthdays. The school had one large room and one large schoolmaster, Mr Palfreyman, who had come from London. He was so well-educated, so cultivated and altogether so surprising a village schoolmaster that the villagers paid him the homage of believing that he had run into trouble in the metropolis, and had fled under an assumed name to the obscurity of Hedingham. Mr Palfreyman was thus invested with an aura of mystery, distinction and supposed raffishness that his own denials, and the testimony of a blameless life amongst them, could never dispel. He was tall, formidable and irascible, with a heavy walrus moustache and piercing blue eyes. He was so strong that he once seized a large boy by the seat of his breeches and lightly threw him out of the school, for ever. His pupils lived in awe of him and in the morning they ran panting, for fear of being late, past the blacksmith's shop, asking, 'Oh, Mr Fisher, has the clock gone to school?' To lend proper dignity to his calling, he wore a long black frock-coat which hung open to show a row of pearl waistcoat buttons and a thick gold watchchain. His plain white shirt had a stiff turned-down collar under which he tucked the wings of a narrow black bow tie so that very little of it showed. The elegance of the wide silk lapels of his frock-coat and of his neatly buttoned black boots was complemented by an embroidered pill-box hat with which, in and out of school, Mr Palfreyman covered his balding head. A local newspaper, the *Lindsey Star*, once described him as 'the respected and energetic schoolmaster of Hedingham'. Respected he undoubtedly was, and he certainly needed to be energetic to teach fifty children without an assistant, and to be willing to increase his burden by accepting pupils below normal school age and well above it, and even from other villages. Harry Parry was one of them. He was seventeen and lived in Kirton Lindsey, four miles away. When he presented himself for admission, Mr Palfreyman said he didn't want anyone so old amongst his young children ; but Harry said that his age didn't matter for he was 'dunce enough'. So the schoolmaster laughed and took him. Harry was always submissive and obedient, though he was even taller and more muscular than his teacher. It was just as well, because Mr Palfreyman told him, 'You're as big as the side of a house ; but I'll thrash you !'

The compulsory age for school attendance was five, but each Fisher child on his fourth birthday was sent off across the Green to start his education. No time was to be lost in relieving his mother and the servant girl of the trouble of looking after him. Nor was it of the least importance that schooling should start at the beginning of an academic year, at the beginning of a term, or even at the beginning of a week. In one schoolroom holding fifty children of both sexes, and of all ages from four to seventeen, tuition was necessarily individual, except for the group activities that were within the competence of them all. They sang together. Many things could be recited or declaimed together, the ignorant being swept along by the accomplished—multiplication tables, the rivers of England in order from the Tweed downwards, the dates of the kings and queens of England, tables of weights and measures, prayers, and poems such as 'The Loss of the Royal George', 'How Horatius held the Bridge', 'The Revenge', and Henry V's speech before Agincourt. Many things could be listened to together—some children understanding, some not—the story of the crusades, the fables of Aesop, the legends of Greece and Rome, Bible stories, chapters from novels that Mr Palfreyman particularly loved, like *The Mill on the Floss*, *The Pickwick Papers*, *Rob Roy*, *Kenilworth*, *Lorna Doone*, and *Westward Ho!* An infant of four might as well be plunged into all that on one day in the revolving sequence as on another.

Apart from the general participatory education, each child had to be taught individually to read, write and do arithmetic by the schoolmaster, or by an older child, sitting at his side and showing him how to do it on a slate. The first lesson was how to hold a slate pencil at the right angle so that it would not make a screech that set the teeth on edge. Slates were cleaned by spitting on them and wiping with an old rag. While some children were being given this particular tuition, the others were set tasks of reading, copying, drawing and writing essays. And the silence of those others was absolute. Mr Palfreyman used a cane, and even if it scarred the personalities of his victims, as some think, it did at least maintain order and allowed those who were capable of learning to become a little educated in what would otherwise have been a bear-garden. The schoolmaster used his stick on girls and boys alike, except that whereas the boys had to bend over and were hit on the behind, the girls were more chastely struck on the outstretched palm. The pupils did not resent it, and their parents supported it. Once Mr Palfreyman caned my Aunt Mary for an offence she had not committed and in anger at being disbelieved she cried, 'I'll tell my mother!' This provoked the schoolmaster to shout, 'I'm your mother, your father, your uncle, your aunt—your everything here!' He then required her to stand on a form and say to the school that she must 'command her tongue and temper'. Having plenty of spirit, Mary refused; so she was caned again. Yet there was no complaint when she went home, and her parents only heard of the double chastisement because her brothers gleefully recounted it at supper, for Mary was her mother's favourite daughter, and disliked.

Apart from slates, paper, pens, ink, pencils, blackboard,

chalk, a few dog-eared books and a cane, the only other school equipment was a harmonium from which the Protean schoolmaster taught the children hymns and folk songs. In remote Lincolnshire, the young with the sensitive ears could absorb the haunting beauty of 'Tallis's Canon', 'As with Gladness Men of Old', 'When I Survey the Wondrous Cross', 'The King of Love My Shepherd is', and 'At Even Ere the Sun was Set'. The secular songs were as splendid— 'When First I Saw Your Face', 'The Oak and the Ash', 'Robin Adair', 'Barbara Allen', 'The Lorelei', 'When Daisies Pied'. From the age of four Henry became addicted to the intoxication of music, the strangest and most incomprehensible of the arts. The hymns they sang were from the *Ancient and Modern*, for Hedingham was a church school. Therefore the catechism had to be known by heart, and once a year the Rector appeared in his frock-coat and high flat-topped felt hat to examine the school in scripture. Then Mr Palfreyman, who otherwise feared no one, edged round behind him so that he could mouth the answers for the duller pupils, for he dared not risk the school being denied its grant from the Church. The Reverend Mr Smith had never married and slept with his maids instead. My grandfather used to say that he gave them 'three services a week'. Consequently, between searching questions on the catechism, the parson cast his eye over the adolescent girls in the back row for likely recruits to his rectory harem.

There were no organized games at Hedingham School and no equipment for play, and none was needed, for in what little time the children had on their hands they were not deprived of physical exercise. There was work at home for them before school, making beds, chopping sticks, feeding pigs and poultry. After school there was work in the fields and gardens. The only opportunities for play at school were in the mid-morning and mid-afternoon breaks, when the schoolmaster left them to themselves and the old traditional games. They played snobs with a bouncing manny stone and five little square stones painted different colours. Those who had marbles produced them. The girls skipped and sang, 'Green shoes and yellow laces, up and down the market places.' There was another game in which they shouted :

'Sheep, sheep, come home !'
'Afraid !'
'What of?'
'The wolf !'

In chasing games, if a child was tired, or 'fagged', he could get respite from pursuit by crossing his first two fingers and calling 'Kings !' Sometimes one had to be chosen to be odd man out—to be the seeker, for example, in a game of hide and seek. Then they stood in a ring and a child recited : 'Eeena meena makka rakka rare rye dommi nakka chikka pokka alla pakka rom pom—push !' At each word he pointed to a boy or girl in turn, including himself. The last child in the recital was thumped in the chest, and dropped out for the next round, and so on until only one remained. It was a laborious way of choosing one out of many ; but it was thought by the stupid to be fair, whereas Henry quickly perceived that the end depended entirely on where you started. So he always volunteered to be the caller.

A school photograph of 1893 shows how well clothed the Hedingham children were. Before the agricultural depression, Lincolnshire used to boast of its small number of paupers, and a survey of 1842 claimed that very few of the workhouses set up under the New Poor Law of 1834 were occupied by more than one-third of the number of inmates for whom they had accommodation. Even in the eighteen nineties, when times were bad, all the Hedingham children came to school in boots, and none was ragged. The boys wore black or dark grey rough worsted suits with short jackets or doublets buttoned high up to the neck, without lapels. Some had high-necked waistcoats too, and a few wore Eton collars, but usually no tie, because the jackets left no room at the neck for a tie to show. Narrow trousers of similar material went down to just below the knee, leaving a gap between the top of the boots and the bottom of the trousers, which was filled by thick black woollen stockings, secured above the knee by elastic garters. A few very young boys had sailor suits, with the trousers again below the knee. Most of the boys had caps, but of no particular pattern. No child, whether boy or girl, wore shoes. It was always boots, laced well up the calf, and the girls' boots tended to be even higher in the leg than the boys'. They too wore black woollen stockings. Their dresses came just below the knee and were high at the neck. Those of the infant girls were completely covered by white cotton pinafores. All but the youngest girls wore hats of various shapes, some of them very large and grand, being decorated with flowers and ribbons. Raincoats were unknown, and overcoats were a luxury for the rich, so both girls and boys needed thick warm clothes which, for economy, they had to wear all the year round. On hot days the boys could shed vests and waistcoats, but they still sweltered in striped flannel shirts and the woollen stockings. The summer smell of warm humanity in the schoolroom was one of my mother's abiding memories of childhood.

The Fisher children ended their schooldays at thirteen and left on whatever day their birthdays fell, because the girls were needed to help their mother at home and the boys to work for their father in his fields. They all left school literate and numerate, as was usual in a village school at the end of the nineteenth century. Indeed, two generations earlier their grandfather, John Fisher, was able to write very correct English by the time he left school at twelve in 1822 in the small village of Whatton. On the other hand, my grandmother said that most of the inhabitants of Redbourne were illiterate when she was a child in the eighteen-fifties. It depended on when a village first acquired a school. Redbourne had to wait until 1840 for the Duke of St Albans to found a school there, whereas James Thompson had endowed a school in Hedingham as early as 1719 and it was rebuilt in 1830 at a cost of £200. So the Fisher children had the good fortune to attend a school not only with a fine head-master, but with a village tradition of nearly two centuries of paying for education and a corresponding respect for it. The charge for each child at Hedingham School had been a penny or two a week until the Government made education free and lowered its value.

John, Robert, George and Mary in no way distinguished themselves at school. They learned to read and write, and to do simple arithmetic, and they remembered some history and geography. George was perhaps a little dull. John, Robert and Mary were bright enough, but not interested in books. The clever ones were James, Matilda and my mother, although Matilda tended to dream her life away immersed in novels about the more fortunate. Her mother said that 'Mattie always took the light end'—but it was for good reason because she was always offered the heavy one. The very clever child was Henry, yet it was James who had the most remarkable gift in the family—a phenomenal memory. He had total recall. Whether it extended to everything he read, I do not know. It certainly applied to everything he was told or did, and in consequence he was the most excruciating talker I ever had the misfortune to hear. Every anecdote was recounted with a wealth of detail that drove a listener mad with impatience for it to end. James never used indirect speech. Every conversation was repeated verbatim as it was spoken, whether last week or forty years ago, including the umms and aahs. In telling of a journey, we had not only the exact route, but every stop on the way, what he ate, how much it cost, and the variety of each tree behind which he made water. He would tell the entire history of a horse, from being foaled to the knacker's yard. The only thing to do when listening to Uncle James was to break in and change the subject. This he bore with serene good nature, and after even a long interval he would complete his sentence and continue. What Mr Palfreyman made of him I never heard, except that he did very well at school. As an adult he read nothing but *Farm, Field and Fireside* and later the *Farmers Weekly*—indeed, he had not the time, for he hardly ever stopped talking. My mother, too, had a capacious memory, but only for poetry. Grandfather used to lay bets amongst his friends that his daughter Fanny could recite Shakespeare, Browning and Tennyson for two hours on end. Being more fond of wagers than of poetry, they always paid up long before she had even started to exhaust her repertoire. In fact, no one could ever bear to discover the full extent of it.

Apart from the peculiar talents of James and Fanny, none of the children could remotely compare with Henry in general intelligence. By the age of nine he had absorbed everything Mr Palfreyman had time to teach him, and thereafter his schooldays were spent as the schoolmaster's unpaid assistant. He sat beside the younger children and provided their individual tuition. They adored him because he was always gay and amusing. Henry had the heavenly gift of believing that everyone liked him; so most people did, and all children without exception. In return for his help Mr Palfreyman gave Henry special coaching in advanced arithmetic now and then in the evenings, but school holidays were very short and his school day was too full and unremitting for the schoolmaster to have much inclination to continue in the evenings. The nearest grammar school was in Brigg but it was too far for Henry to walk there daily and his father had neither the ability nor the inclination to pay boarding fees. It was the Reverend Mr Smith, a brilliant classical scholar, who could have given Henry the further education he deserved, but he did not offer to do so, and perhaps it was in the end to Henry's advantage that the task was left to Uncle Charlie Rudkin. Nevertheless, the parson was to have so important an influence on Henry's life that I can justify a digression to explain how Charles Smith, of whom more might have been expected, became the Rector of Hedingham.

In writing now about the Rector I must enter the caveat that I can only tell of provincial life towards the end of the nineteenth century as it has been described to me by my relatives who lived then. No doubt they were by temperament not inclined to understate, and may even have exaggerated, the level of rural fornication and adultery; but according to them, the hedgerows, woods, barns, and even bedrooms, heaved with both to a degree that is not normally associated with the adjective Victorian. The participants in the general Lincolnshire saturnalia ranged, if my informants are to be believed, through all ranks of society; and the highest in the country did not scruple to take their pleasure with the lowest, nor the lowest with the highest. For example, I have mentioned that my grandmother was the daughter of the Redbourne blacksmith. He had a journeyman, George Harrison, who was notoriously addicted to the nobility and gentry and was once discovered by my infant grandmother *flagrante delicto* on a heap of straw in his master's barn with Lady Mary from the great house. And that house was one of the two principal seats of the Duke of

St Albans who had the good fortune to be descended from a natural son of Charles II by 'Eleanor Gwynn'—as *Burke's Peerage* frequently and respectfully calls her. So I must make clear that even if during the reign of Queen Victoria the urban bourgeoisie led virtuous lives, my relatives saw little sign that virtue prevailed in the villages of Lincolnshire, and it certainly did not in the Rectory of Hedingham.

Mr Smith did not enter the ministry of the Church of England on account of any great religious conviction or sense of vocation. In the course of taking his statutory services he recited the Creed with the voice of assurance, but he certainly did not believe in the resurrection of the body, nor was he persuaded that God the Son had been begotten by the Holy Ghost on the Virgin Mary. The impossibilities of the Christian faith, that so appealed to Sir Thomas Browne, had no charms for Charles Smith. He had been drawn into the Established Church as a young man by the rhythms of its prayer book, by the beauty of its music, by the splendour of its buildings, and by the prospect of rising in a decorous way through its hierarchy to an old stone deanery in some placid cathedral close—Salisbury for preference. As a scholar of Eton and of King's College, Cambridge, with a fine voice and a good presence, a deanery had seemed a modest ambition ; but there was nothing else that Smith had particularly wanted to do. So after two indolent firsts in classics, he entered an Oxford theological college, and as soon as he was ordained priest he accepted an invitation to return to King's College as chaplain. There he entertained undergraduates to Madeira, and intoned the chapel services with an impeccable sense of pitch and an exquisite appreciation of the cadences of Elizabethan English. Then after a few years it happened, in the Church of England way, that one evening the Provost took him aside after a college feast and said, 'My dear Smith, we have fortuitously rather a good living vacant in Lincolnshire. Or perhaps fortuitously is not the word, for they say, if I recall correctly, that the late incumbent killed himself. The living is not by any means one of the recognized steps on the ladder, or whatever one ascends in the Anglican Church ; but think about it, Smith, think about it ! Rowlands will give you the precise details—it may be in Norfolk ; but I am credibly informed that we have a living vacant somewhere. Of course, Smith, we should be sorry to lose you because you don't mumble, but I thought I ought to tell you. Think about it, my dear Smith. Please do.'

Smith did not think seriously about it at all, and it was only out of idle curiosity he went to see a Lincolnshire parish with a stipend of two thousand pounds a year and the scene of a clerical suicide. For the first reason alone it was a comparative rarity. The visit was his undoing, for the widow of the late incumbent was still, by arrangement with the churchwardens, living in the Rectory as caretaker, and she had retained four of the servants, amongst whom was a rather beautiful seventeen-year-old girl called Bridget Atkinson, of a Hedingham family distantly related to mine. From the age of fourteen Smith had been troubled by the flesh but had been too fearful and shy to make carnal over-tures to any woman, until in his second year at Cambridge he had joined a party of rich young men who regularly bribed their bedmakers not to report them absent when they went off by train for a night in London. There Smith quenched temporarily his sensual thirst in a discreet and expensive brothel where the girls were young. Thenceforth, as an undergraduate, as a theological student and later as a college chaplain, he returned at least monthly to the same house. The unbridled surrender to sensuality he enjoyed there was so totally outside his concept of Christian marriage that he could see no release from his bondage in matrimony. It seemed inconceivable that a sacrament could license a husband and wife to abandon themselves to the flesh in a way that was natural to his own desperate sexuality and had been reflected so shamelessly by the inclination or training of his hired partners. Matrimony, therefore, for him was worse than no solution. A wife could not be expected to meet his needs, and to substitute adultery for fornication would only increase the measure of his ecclesiastical sin and risk.

25

Consequently, Smith was a bachelor when the widow invited him to stay the night at Hedingham Rectory, and Bridget Atkinson was the housemaid who preceded him up the winding oak staircase to show him his room. He could only be reminded of other girls, no more lovely, who had walked before him with swinging hips and backward smiling glances along other corridors leading to other rooms with large beds. Bridget stayed to light his fire, to unpack his bag, and to pour out water from the ewer into his wash-bowl, while he sat on the bed watching every movement she made. As she came to turn down the sheets he rose to his feet and asked, much too quietly, 'If I became the rector here, would you stay and work for me?' Bridget turned quickly and glanced at him. Village girls seldom reached the age of seventeen in innocence, and Smith's eyes had, though he didn't know it, long surrendered their chastity to his experience. Perhaps at that moment Bridget did not conclude explicitly what working for the Reverend Mr Smith might involve, but she was at least conscious that her answer was of greater importance to the questioner than the mere availability of a housemaid in a locality where there was no shortage. She hesitated and Smith sensed that he had been too precipitate. 'Of course,' he added, 'I should want to employ the four of you. I have no wife to arrange servants for me and I suppose you all know how to run the place.' 'Oh yes, sir,' replied Bridget, seeing an advantage for her fellow servants, 'and I shall be pleased to stay if the others will.' It happened that the others also were pleased to work for him, so Smith resigned his chaplaincy and accepted the gift of a cure of souls, with substantial temporalities, from the hands of the Provost and Fellows of King's College, Cambridge, for no better reason than that he ached to employ Bridget Atkinson as his housemaid.

The Rectory of Hedingham was a by-way leading off the main roads to preferment in the Church of England. Smith would remain there unnoticed till he died unless his College happened to remember him when they needed a Dean ; and in fact they forgot him. Nevertheless the obscurity of

Hedingham had its compensations. Although Smith was himself a rich man, the addition of two thousand pounds a year was noticeable, and the seduction of Bridget was easy. In church she listened to his beautifully modulated voice caressing the words of the English Prayer Book. She wondered at the calm, lucid fluency of his sermons, and did not much trouble herself to distinguish the love he preached from the love his eyes suggested he might wish to practise. Bridget was impressed, too, by the Rector's ability to play both the violin and the piano at speeds and with an assurance that seemed to her incredible ; and when, while making his bed, she peeped at the books by his bedside, she found that her employer read himself to sleep with what, cook assured her, was Latin and Greek. Although the parson was considerably less than good-looking, Bridget fell in love, as women are accustomed to do, with his distinction. He was intelligent, cultivated, rich and well-bred, so his housemaid had no chance against a campaign of seduction that was as leisurely and discreet as it was nicely calculated.

Before long the Rector was confident enough to go in his nightshirt up to Bridget's attic bedroom, where he lay with her in the darkness in her narrow bed. Thereafter she was invited to his own large candle-lit room and they made love with great regularity and delight. Yet even in the Rector's bedroom, Bridget called him 'Sir'. Her employer remained as far beyond the reach of a Christian name when he lay naked in her arms as when he was clad in frock-coat or surplice. It never occurred to her to call him 'Charles', nor did she ever seriously suppose that he might marry her. So when she was later courted by George Anderson, one of her distant cousins, she accepted his advances and, in the village tradition, she started to make love with him too, out in the woods in summer and on straw in barns in winter. By the same tradition, when she became pregnant he married her. It was well known that the parson took her to his bed and that there was ambiguity about the paternity of the child, but the dowry of two hundred gold sovereigns that Smith provided made Bridget an heiress. It was as much as she could have earned virtuously in thirty years. After Bridget's wedding the parson recruited another housemaid, and the sequence of seduction, enjoyment, pregnancy, dowry and marriage was repeated for her and several others. By the time that Henry Fisher first recited the catechism in Hedingham School to the visiting Rector, the system had been working for many years, and Bridget was one of Henry's more distant middle-aged aunts. The succession of girls made no trouble for Smith because he was kind and generous to them and they invariably liked him. The village made no trouble because the parson was charming and gentle. Masters slept with their maids. The text, 'Sleep not for ye know not when the Master cometh,' had long been, amongst housemaids, a tired jest; and if Smith's position as a cleric was exceptional, he was also unusual in his popularity. The village wished him no harm, because if Smith were to leave they might find themselves with a Rector as proud and arrogant as Mr Harrison of Redbourne, known by my grandmother as 'the old hunx', who was both virtuous and detested. Of course, Smith's immorality was talked of over port and coffee cups in Minster Yard, but Lincolnshire had many parsons whose lives were in various ways not beyond criticism, and in the absence of complaint or open scandal the Bishop thought it sensible to turn a blind eye upon Smith's only rumoured and at least heterosexual transgressions. Eventually, when he was seventy-five, Smith in atonement made an honest woman of his twenty-year-old cook, and was so delighted to have a legitimate child that he had water brought from the River Jordan for its baptism. Then not long afterwards he died, leaving his wife a handsome annuity and his son a fortune of seventy thousand pounds.

So that was how Charles Smith became, thanks to Aunt Bridget, the Rector of Hedingham. Henry told me the story of her seduction with as great an affection for her seducer as relish for the subject, because it was the Rector who taught him to play the violin, and no one else in Hedingham could have done so. A fiddle came Henry's way because his father when a young man had bought one to play simple tunes, like 'The Keel Row', by ear and without any formal teaching. When Henry was five, his father saw that he wanted to have a try himself, and let him. He tuned the fiddle for him, showed him how to hold it and how to bow it, and then went out into the blacksmith's shop to escape the consequences. However, his mother had to suffer them, and they were severe, for Henry could never thereafter leave the instrument alone. Eventually she banished him to the cowshed and while he was there one summer afternoon it happened that the Rector was walking past and heard him. Of course, he had to peep through a crack in the door to see who it was, if only because one or two of the intervals were surprisingly in tune. As he watched, he recognized a child whom he had already earmarked for his choir on his visits to the school when, as they sang their hymns and folk songs, he walked up and down in front of the children locating the good voices.

As he watched through the cowshed door, Smith resolved to take the young Fisher under his wing. Although the boy held his fiddle wrongly, he held it in a way that expressed his potential command over it. He struck it boldly with his bow, undeterred by the disastrous noise. He was not afraid of the instrument as so many are who try, hopelessly, to play on tensed gut with rosined horsehair. Eventually the parson went into the shed, took the fiddle, tuned it, and set off on Tartini's 'Devil's Trill' Sonata. Henry was so astonished at the sound of it, and so mortified by the difference between his music and the Rector's, that he burst into tears ; and the howls of the child and the laughter of the Devil mingled until the Rector was satisfied that he had driven home the message that there were tremendous and overwhelming sounds to be made, if only one knew how. Then he led the boy round to his mother and arranged with her that Henry should go to the Rectory every Monday afternoon after school for tea and a violin lesson. The Rector lent him a half-sized violin, and within two years Henry was playing well enough to be regarded in the village as an infant prodigy—which he was not, as Smith was well aware. He knew that Henry's musical talent was similar to his own. Study and practise as he might, the child could never become more than a very good amateur or, if he were foolish enough to try to earn a living with his bow, a second-rate professional. The Rector taught Henry assiduously for years and brought him to a high level of skill, but always cooled his pupil's enthusiasm with the wise advice that it was better to play 'le violon d'Ingres' than the first fiddle in a municipal orchestra.

The Rector had been so adept at Eton and Cambridge in impressing examiners, that he set little store by academic attainment, but he could never free himself from reproach for having abandoned the world of learning for the sensuality of Hedingham Rectory. Thus, while he would be troubled to teach Bridget Atkinson's talented nephew to play the violin, he could not bring himself to teach him Latin and Greek. The juxtaposition of associations would have been too conflicting and painful. Also, Charles Smith was, like most of the clergy, a snob. He had no great wish to see gifted village children pushed unnaturally into Oxford and Cambridge. So up to the age of thirteen Henry's education depended on what he was taught at school and on the books that came his way. Fortunately, although he was not stocking a capacious mind with classical history, he was generating a head of steam. Ambition was, of course, fostered at home, but Henry was brought up in a total environment that strengthened his early conviction that he was outside the common run of humanity and a natural candidate for life's favours. The example of his Anderson and Kirby relatives encouraged this attitude of mind. Apart from the parson and a small squire who lived on the edge of the village, they were the principal figures in Hedingham, with a high opinion of themselves and a ruthless contempt for the unsuccessful. They owed their existence to the absence in Hedingham of a great rural potentate to own and dominate the village, like the Duke of St Albans in Redbourne.

The Fisher children used to visit their prosperous

Hedingham uncles at handsome farmhouses, with the buildings discreetly huddled to one side. The houses had ten or more bedrooms and there were a couple of maids in the kitchen. The gardens were beautifully tended, the lawns were smooth and the hedges well clipped; but these Andersons and Kirbys were yeomen, not gentlemen. None of them owned more than two or three hundred acres and they all worked in their own fields. A gentleman-farmer never did that, even at harvest, even with the bailiffs coming up the drive. Financial death before dishonour was the gentry's motto, whereas these yeomen were still working to buy enough land to have mottoes. Robert Anderson was a little ahead of the others in that pursuit. He lived at the largest establishment, the Priory, where Henry and the others were sometimes invited at midday for Sunday dinner. Robert was huge and patriarchal, weighing twenty stone, with a red face and black side whiskers. He presided with great formality and solemnity over a table invariably set out on Sunday with roast sirloin of beef—a great luxury for the Fishers—followed by groat pudding with currants in it. He was a very grand farmer and kept a governess for his many daughters. One branch of the Kirbys had a similar establishment on the road to Snitterby and another lived in a handsome house on a corner near the church in Snitterby itself; but of them all the Fishers preferred the noisy Back Lane Andersons in Hedingham, where John Anderson's mild rule allowed them to romp and shout through the house in a way that was utterly forbidden at home.

Andersons and Kirbys had intermarried with each other for generations and with Maitlands, Hiles, Rudkins and Atkinsons. Consequently, practically all the farmers and master-craftsmen in Hedingham were closely enough related to my grandfather to be regarded as his cousins, and that is how they sometimes addressed each other. Henry was able to call at least a dozen men in the village 'uncle', and these men and their families constituted an inter-related group of rural bourgeoisie with a well-defined sense of hierarchy. Freehold farmers were at the top and self-employed artisans were at the bottom. There was no place within it for a labourer, nor for a journeyman who worked for a master other than his father. Body-servants were utterly beyond the pale. A younger son of these Hedingham families would have died before becoming a footman, and he would, for shame, leave the village to work elsewhere if he had to work for a wage. All this bred a splendid independence, self-reliance and sense of being an élite which Henry grew up to share. It was villages in East Anglia like Hedingham that bred Cromwell's Ironsides. On the other hand, the social structure and the diversity of land-ownership did not make for a pretty village. Trees had been cut down because they shaded cottage gardens. There were no stately avenues laid through the village on their way to neoclassical gate houses. Everyone had built as he liked, and the houses in the village streets observed neither a common architectural style, nor a building line. They were like a very irregular row of teeth, some forward, some backward, some missing, and all different.

Redbourne, only three miles away, was a village entirely unlike Hedingham. It was shrouded in trees, for no one but the Duke had authority to cut them down. Every house and cottage was built of stone in a consistent architectural style, and most of them carried the seigniorial arms. The school was approached through a Gothic stone archway, and the blacksmith's shop, let to my great-grandfather, looked like a Greek temple. The portico was a colonnade of pillars surmounted by a triangular pediment with a large white stallion carved in wood mounted on the apex. The horse was rearing on its hind legs, with forefeet pawing the air, as if stung by a hornet. The main gates to the mansion were set in a stone archway flanked by a pair of identical lodge houses, presenting a total façade designed to repel invaders, with cruciform embrasures for archers and battlements overhead for other defenders—notwithstanding that the entire structure could be outflanked at either end by breaking through a hedge. At the highest point of the Gothic gateway, stood a carved stone lion passant guardant on three legs, with tail and one forefoot elegantly uplifted. Splendours of that kind, and particularly the charming *jeu d'esprit* of the blacksmith's shop, made Redbourne a very beautiful village ; and it was kept so because the Duke owned every building in it except the church and the rectory, and he owned them, too, in the sense that he had the right of presentation to the benefice. So everyone said, 'Yes, Your Grace', and 'No, Your Grace', and men touched their forelocks and the women and children did curtsy bobs. Henry often walked over to visit his grand-father, and if he was outside the blacksmith's shop when the sound of a coaching horn was heard, Thomas Millson would push him indoors because it heralded the approach of the Duke in his coach-and-four with outriders in front and foot-men standing up behind, one of them blowing the horn. Henry was spared the indignity of touching his forelock, but Thomas's tenancy depended on his staying outside and making the gesture of subservience. Mr Harrison, the hated Rector, expected the same deference, and there was a tale of a joiner who, in the time of the ninth Duke, went to live in Redbourne but whose wife refused to curtsy to the Rector. He complained to the Duke, who summoned the joiner to see him. The man said that his wife did as she pleased and that he could not control her genuflexions. So the Duke had a word with the woman, who not only flatly refused to curtsy to the Rector but to the Duke as well. She would, she said, 'only bow her knee to her Maker'. This religious zeal commended itself no more to the Duke than it did to the Rector, and the joiner was obliged to take his family and his stiff-legged wife out of the village again, because the Duke owned the roof over his head and the roof over the head of everyone who might give him employment.

Yet the ninth Duke, as dukes went, was a kindly and enlightened man. He sat on the Liberal benches in the House of Lords, and cared for his tenants and loved their children. His charge for a cottage, a cow and three acres of land was two shillings a week. Old widows and spinsters had almshouses and cottages for one shilling a year, and when they went annually to the Hall to pay their rent, they were given a good dinner. The Duchess, too, was as greatly loved in the village for her benefactions as she was despised in the county for her origins. Harriet had been born in a ditch, the daughter of a travelling actress. Then she followed her mother's profession until she married Thomas Coutts, the banker, who obligingly died not long afterwards, leaving her so rich a widow that the impecunious ninth Duke of St Albans quickly snapped her up, to the loud acclaim of his creditors. However, the Lincolnshire nobility and gentry were less well pleased, because a duchess enjoyed precedence over all other ladies in the county, who had to defer at the Stuff Ball to a woman who had not only been dropped in a ditch by a wandering actress but laughed about it. Even the Right Honourable John, Earl Brownlow, His Majesty's Lieutenant, Custos Rotulorum and Vice Admiral of Lincolnshire, whose not so remote ancestors had been little better than sheep stealers, would not allow his wife to be in the same room as the Duchess lest she should be obliged to bow to her.

Thomas Millson was a devout member of the Established Church and, though he disliked touching his forelock, he bent his neck to the not very harsh yoke of the Duke of St Albans with the humility that was recommended twice weekly to his parishioners by the ducal nominee from the pulpit of Redbourne Church. Everyone in the village went to hear the Christian message because non-attendance at any of the Sunday services brought a visit from the Rector to demand an explanation. Too many absences without the excuse of sickness would lead him to complain to the Duke and, after unheeded warnings, the offender would be expelled from the village. Thus Redbourne set standards of church attendance that were an example to the whole county, while the Sermon on the Mount continued, as in Hedingham where Nonconformity was rife, to be regarded for all practical purposes as nonsense—particularly by the Rector. The Duke, too, was more concerned that his tenants should till his fields than consider the lilies, but the upper classes were no worse than the villagers except in their calculated lip-service to religion. The villagers themselves respected only strength, trampled on weakness, and made no pretence to do otherwise. The men beat their wives, their children and their animals with little mercy and even less compunction. Most of the inhabitants of Redbourne were unbelievably clownish, brutish and cruel, and only a small minority were literate. Thomas was one of them, and used to read the newspapers aloud to gatherings of men in the blacksmith's shop.

Above all, Thomas was kind and gentle and was adored by his grandchildren. He had time to listen endlessly, to take the children for long walks in the woods, and to tell tales of his childhood in Long Ludford, with stories of the Battle of Waterloo that he had heard from an uncle who had fought in the artillery under Sir George Wood. Thomas talked 'thee' and 'thou' to those he loved and was himself entirely lovable, though no beauty. His lower lip stuck out, according to my Aunt Matilda, 'like an old ewe chewing turnips'. He had thin grey hair and a little whiskery growth all round the edges of his face. His hands, hair, clothes and boots all had to be fastidiously neat and clean, and his love of good order in everything about him, including his house, was inherited by my grandmother. Thomas loved animals, and his pets included cats, dogs, parrots, lambs and, best of all, a duck. He found her as a duckling in a drain and brought her home in his pocket and kept her for many years. She was called Jane and slept in an outhouse, getting in by squeezing through a crevice long after the less privileged poultry had been locked up in the fowlhouse. Jane waddled down the street behind my great-grandfather when he went to the shop. She followed him through the churchyard when he went, as parish clerk, to light the church furnace on Saturday night, and to wind the church clock. Thomas would nurse her in the kitchen by the fire, and take her out in the evening for a walk at her own slow pace through the village. People used to say, 'There goes Millson and his duck.' If he was away from home she looked out for his return and greeted him with affectionate quacking. Now and then he walked the six miles to Brigg to spend an evening with his boon companion, Isaac Spike, in the public houses. Jane would swim up and down the beck waiting for him to come back. Then, as soon as she heard his unsteady steps, she swam under the bridge and, as he crossed over, quacked loudly and joyfully to mark his return, disclosing to the village that the blacksmith had been out drinking again. So her greeting was met with an ungrateful volley of stones and curses. Jane was functional as well, and laid eggs and sat on them and brought off her ducklings ; but Thomas never kept any of them to maturity to rival Jane. Eventually she paid the price for her nocturnal activities and the fox ate her. Shortly after Jane's death, a threshing machine was brought into Thomas's yard for repair and in the drum was a little chicken, so he kept it ; but his kindness was unrequited and it wouldn't stay at home. Always it was going off to Hall's Farm, so one day Thomas went to retrieve it for the last time. Back home he wrung its neck, cooked it and ate it. So he was only sentimental up to a point. Indeed, although he loved his cats, he couldn't resist the pleasure of watching a fight, and he would provoke them to squabble whenever he could. If they were asleep on the hearthrug, he would pick up one of them and drop it on the other's back simply to see the fur fly.

His grandfather's cats were Henry's first close acquaintance with the true felis domestica, the idle and pampered aristocracy of the fireside. At home in Hedingham the cats were half-wild and lived in the outhouses as ratcatchers. They hunted their own food, apart from an occasional dish of milk, and they never came into the house. Surplus kittens were ruthlessly drowned in a bucket as soon as they revealed their existence by staggering out of the hiding place their careful mother had chosen for their nursery. Even Thomas Millson's cats had to hunt for their own meat, for he, like the other villagers, had none to spare except bits of bacon, the raw giblets of an occasional fowl, or the boiled lights when he killed a pig. Otherwise all the food he ever gave his cats was milk, household scraps, and bread and gravy. But his cats lay on the hearthrug in winter, and in summer they followed the sun so religiously round his living-room that he reckoned he could tell the time of day from where they were lying ; and not only did he use them as a sundial but he drew edifying comparisons for his grandson's benefit between the feline and the canine creations. 'When thou grows up, bairn,' he used to say, 'don't thou be a dog, like me. I've wagged my tail o'er much for what I've been given by the folk up there'—he inclined his head in the direction of Redbourne Hall—'but I've never, thank God, barked and bitten for them like some I could name !' Henry knew that his grandfather's piety precluded any thought that he was aiming a shaft in the Rector's direction. His target was, in fact, James Clayton, the Duke's agent. 'Nay, bairn, thou must be a cat, like thy father. Beholden to no one. Go thy own way. Let others be. Come when thou pleases, and go when thou wants. Scratch if they pull thy tail, and always be ready to catch thee's own dinner.' Not that Thomas disliked dogs. He had so overflowing an affection for all God's creatures that it embraced even the dogs he identified with, and so rightly despised.

Thomas Millson had four children by his first wife Caroline, whom he had met in 1847 in Great Ponton near Grantham when he was tramp-blacksmith. He had been apprenticed to his father in Ludford, but there was insufficient work there for the two of them when he came out of his articles, so he went to the Grantham area because many large estates lay in that locality, and also because the Great North Road ran through. A hundred and sixty post-horses were kept in Grantham, sixty at Colsterworth, and up to a hundred at Long Bennington. So there was plenty of work for an itinerant blacksmith along that stretch of the road. However, as soon as Thomas and Caroline married, he settled in Hedingham as a journeyman to John Maitland, the master blacksmith. John worked in his own forge, but he sent his journeyman, rightly so named, out daily to the neighbouring big farmers who maintained their own blacksmith shops. Thomas spent two days a week at Hall's and two days at Campbell's, also near Redbourne, and the other two days of the week at Peter Kirby's farm in Snitterby. He walked to and from these places of work daily.

My grandmother, Bessie, was their first child, born in 1849. Then, while still living in Hedingham, they had James, Thomas and George. The birth of the fourth child so weakened Caroline that she contracted consumption and infected her baby. My grandmother was five at the time and wrote this when she was eighty-seven :

> I remember the poor little thing. He took his mother's complaint at six months. I used to nurse him for hours on a little stool. He didn't cry—just made a little moan. I remember him so well and I remember following him to the grave. They took him up in a donkey cart—mother couldn't walk. She sat in the cart and we walked. I remember taking father's hand and walking with him.

Caroline died of consumption shortly after the baby, when she was only thirty-two. In the same year Thomas was given a tenancy of the blacksmith's shop and house in Redbourne by the Duke of St Albans. So the widower moved there with his three orphan children in 1856. Most of the belongings had preceded them in an open waggon, but because it was raining Dickie Ducker the Hedingham carrier, took the family in a covered cart with Thomas's most prized possession, his grandfather clock. In Redbourne, Thomas engaged a housekeeper aged twenty, called Rachael, to look after him, his three children, and a lodger-blacksmith called George Harrison, whose sexual conquests amongst the nobility I have already mentioned. One of Rachael's duties was to get up at six every Sunday morning to bake bread. As the parish clerk, Thomas also rose early on Sundays to stoke the church furnace and to ring the bell to summon the villages to communion at eight. When he came home after taking the sacrament, Rachael provided him with a breakfast of home-cured ham, fresh eggs and freshly baked bread. This practice continued for the eleven years Rachael remained Thomas's housekeeper, until my grandmother left home at the age of sixteen to go into service in

Lincoln. Thomas then fell at last into the common error of marrying his housekeeper. Thereafter he could rise with an untroubled conscience from Rachael's bed to summon the village to Divine Service, but there was no more baking of bread at dawn on Sunday mornings.

Even as a housekeeper, Rachael had enjoyed an easy life compared with many. Her cousin Mary went to be housekeeper for Mr Brierley, the Redbourne schoolmaster, whose wife also died young of consumption, leaving him with many children. Mary's job was to cook and clean the schoolhouse in the morning, to act as 'school-governess', or assistant teacher, in the afternoon, and to act as ducal sempstress in the evening. The ninth Duke had, with Coutts' money, provided the school and the family still called the tune. All the new napery, linen and towels of the noble household were taken over from the Hall to the school for the girls to embroider them with the St Albans' crest; but the children did so bad a job on the embroidery by day, that the school governess had to unpick it by night and work the detail correctly. She did this by paraffin lamplight and damaged her eye-sight to the extent that she went blind and lost her employment. Her wages had been ten pounds a year with no provision for old age and Mary ended her unhappy days in the workhouse. Mr Brierley had not married her because she was plain. Instead he had cast his eyes upon my grandmother who had been his favourite pupil until she left school at the age of thirteen. Then she stayed at home with her father, and the schoolmaster was a constant visitor to the house because he kept the blacksmith's accounts. For three years he watched her grow into womanhood, and when she was sixteen Henry Brierley was prompted by the clamour of the flesh to propose that they should marry, although he was thirty years older than she. Female pupils are sadly liable to become infatuated with their masters, as we know by the delighted testimony of pedagogues so diverse as ski-instructors and professors at the Royal Academy of Music. My grandmother was no exception and nursed a deep *tendresse* for her former master.

However, I do not know whether it was her own good sense, or her father's advice, or the thought of becoming the ducal sempstress that prevailed, but Mr Brierley was rejected. He had to content himself with a promise that Bessie would call her first son Henry after him, and even there he was disappointed. When the time came for the pledge to be implemented, my grandfather was not tamely prepared to accept a name that was foreign to the family without enquiring why his wife so much desired it. Of course, when the story of Mr Brierley was told he would not agree to the proposed perpetuation of his memory—it was enough for grandfather himself always to remind his wife of the son of the Town Clerk of Lincoln, without his eldest son continually reminding her of the master of Redbourne School. The objection was maintained for the second son, but by the time the third arrived grandfather gave up the struggle, and Henry Fisher belatedly fulfilled his mother's pledge. Thereafter the name Henry spread like an epidemic through the family, until now almost a dozen of my grandmother's descendants, including my brother, bear unconscious testimony to the charms of the Redbourne schoolmaster.

Thomas Millson remained the Redbourne blacksmith until 1893 when Henry was eleven. In that year Thomas's wife Rachael died and he became a widower for the second time. He was then seventy-one and had no wish to hire another housekeeper, nor to live in Redbourne alone. So it was arranged, to my grandmother's delight, that he should retire and go to live with her in Hedingham. What commended the arrangement to my grandfather was Thomas's willingness to devote his life's savings of two hundred and fifty pounds to a joint farming venture. With this accession of capital, my grandfather was now able to commit himself wholly to farming. He sold the blacksmith's house and shop to Steeper Dickson, his journeyman, and contributed the proceeds of sale to the partnership, together with fifty pounds lent to him by Annie Fisher, who was his first cousin once removed. Annie and her younger sister Olive, although they thoroughly disliked each other, lived together in Nottingham, in spinsterhood but not in chastity. Cousin Olly was a dressmaker, whereas Cousin Annie was lazy and lived on money inherited from her mother's family, who made it by retail trade and extreme parsimony. Fortunately Annie was generous. She gladly lent my grandfather her body whenever opportunity arose and when he asked for a loan of twenty pounds she simply replied, 'Why not fifty?' So fifty it was, and grandfather diligently paid her back with interest and with passion.

The partners deposited their joint capital of three hundred and fifty pounds with the Lincoln and Lindsey Banking Company Limited in Brigg, and took a tenancy of the whole of the Glebe Farm in Hedingham, of which grandfather had previously farmed only twelve acres. It had a good farmhouse and a hundred acres of poor land. Thomas brought with him his horse, two red and white cows, his old dog, his old cats and a number of useful chattels. Amongst them was a bow-fronted mahogany chest of drawers, an elegant rocking-chair with a canework back, a Windsor armchair, a grandfather clock made by Jonathan White of Kirton Lindsey with a painted face decorated with shepherdesses and roses, and a set of chairs and a table which, if they were not by Chippendale as Thomas supposed, were nevertheless of high quality and very beautiful. This furniture and his numerous pieces of china and bric-a-brac helped to furnish the quite large farmhouse called the Glebe, into which the family moved. It was of well-weathered scarlet Lincolnshire brick, with a red pan-tiled roof and dormer windows. It stood four-square and dignified amongst the farm buildings, and its charm so caught Henry's imagination that it became the prototype of the house in which he always thereafter wanted to live. The façade was symmetrical, with the front door between two windows on the ground floor; then three windows on the next floor and three windows above them in the roof. The brickwork was covered up to the eaves in white Gloire de Dijon roses, and the front windows looked out upon a lawn flanked by two old yew trees that stood sentinel at each end of the house and had grown higher than the ridge of the roof. Children could lean out of the attic windows and pick the poisonous berries. Beyond the lawn was a long garden stretching down to the village street, bounded by tall yew hedges and full of fruit trees and box-edged walks.

The Glebe had a very large stone-flagged kitchen in a wing at the rear of the house, with a high ceiling from which hams and flitches of bacon were hung. The general cooking was done on a coal-fired iron range but there was also an old brick oven which was heated with faggots of wood called 'kids'. The wood was burned in the oven itself; then the hot ashes were raked out and the oven retained its heat long enough to bake pork pies to perfection, followed by the bread, which needed a slightly lower temperature. A flight of stone steps led down from the kitchen into the cream dairy which, for coolness, was below ground level. Here a row of pancheons—large red earthenware bowls with black glazed interior surfaces—stood filled with milk on the brick floor waiting for the cream to rise. When the cream had risen, a finger was run round the edge of the pancheon, and a sile or sieve was slipped underneath the creamy mantle and then lifted to drain away the milk—hence the Lincolnshire expression 'siling with rain'. The butter churn was operated in the cream dairy, and from time to time my grandfather would go down the steps and take the maid from the rear as she bent over her work. It was typical of him that he should not want anyone in his employment to be idle, even while gratifying his carnal desires. If he had a predilection for the steps leading down into the cream dairy, for the children the most fascinating feature of the kitchen was a very deep cupboard sunk into the wall, with no door, into which everything not wanted, such as old clothes, was flung. It was the perfect place in which to hide and was known as 'the Oblivion', and sometimes as 'the Glory Hole'. Also leading off the kitchen was a pantry with a window looking straight out on to the crewyard, which adjoined the cowhouse. It was a walled enclosure with paved edges into which all the manure was thrown and in which

43

the cattle were impounded on their way to and from milking so that they should bestow their urine and droppings upon the straw. The characteristic feature of a true Lincolnshire crewyard was that it should be situated immediately outside the pantry window which, in consequence, had to be protected from flies by planting an elderberry tree close to it. Although the outlook from the pantry window was unsalubrious, the kitchen window looked out upon an orchard behind the house that was planted with apples and damsons. In the spring it was alive with blossom and young chicks and ducklings. Beyond it was the paddock with a large pond that on one occasion was teeming with eels. Overnight it filled so solid with them that they were even lying on the bank. Grandfather allowed everyone in the village to come into the paddock, and they pulled out the eels with rakes. Even so, the supply was not exhausted and the survivors departed, as suddenly as they had arrived, overland on their way to the Ancholme, the Humber, the North Sea, the Atlantic, and their breeding grounds in the Sargasso.

In the kitchen the young children had their meals with the servant girl, standing round the plain scrubbed top of the deal table. Good manners were imposed by all upon each other—no elbows, for example, out sideways. If differences of opinion arose and voices were raised, quiet was soon restored by intervention from the living-room where their elders ate in greater state. This room was the largest in the house, being more than twenty feet along, but it had a low ceiling. The doorway from the hall was so low that when the children grew older Robert, the tallest, was able to rest his chin on the top of the living-room door as he opened it, to survey the people inside ; and even my mother grew enough to be able to herald her approach into the living-room by lightly kicking the underside of the door lintel. The window, with starchy white lace curtains and pots of red geraniums, looked out on the front garden. In the middle of the room there was a large dining-table, and the only other furniture was a number of Windsor chairs, a horsehair sofa, a Mason and Hamlin mechanical organ, and a Collard and Collard upright piano with fretted front lined with green baize and fitted with two brass candle sconces. Everything in the room, and indeed in the whole house, shone and sparkled with cleanliness and polish, and here a stiff white linen cloth was spread on the table for midday dinner, eaten on hot gleaming blue-ringed plates by grandfather, grandmother, Thomas Millson and the older children. The knives and forks were of steel, with bone handles, and since the steel was not stainless it had to be cleaned with rough abrasives which wore the knives very thin, and as sharp as razors. When dinner was over Thomas and my grandmother went upstairs for their afternoon rest, and the room was prepared for the evening. The hearthrug was put down and the table was covered with a heavy green chenille cloth with an ornamental fringe of tassels, and a paraffin lamp was set in the middle ready for nightfall.

Across the entrance hall was the sitting-room, furnished with a sofa and chairs covered in matching grass-green plush velvet. There was little else in this room except a bookcase and a cabinet for displaying china, seashells, and other *objets de vertu*. The sitting-room was used only on solemn occasions, and was my grandmother's greatest joy. The entrance hall had a short flight of wide shallow stairs leading to a landing on which stood Thomas Millson's clock. This first landing was only a few steps up from the ground floor and gave access to a small bedroom over the cream dairy which, as I have explained, was below ground level. From the first landing, the staircase reversed direction and went up to the main landing at first floor level. Grandmother laid strips of white drugget down the centre of the stairs to save wear on the stair carpet, but the drugget was so clean that the children never dared tread on it, so they used the exposed edges of the carpet on either side instead. A narrower and steeper staircase led up to a couple of attic bedrooms, while the third was reached by another staircase from the kitchen because it was for the farm labourers. In all there were eight bedrooms, and some of them were floored with stone slabs, so the timbers of the house must have been very strong. The main bedrooms had lovely cast-iron fireplaces but fires were never lit in them except in case of illness or for particularly important visitors. The windows had blinds and white lace curtains that ran freely on mahogany rings on mahogany poles but were usually drawn back to let in the light. The dressing-tables were covered in white spotted muslin and the mirrors on them had lace curtains draped over the top and fastened at the centre with a ribbon tied in a bow. All the family's beds had white ruffled valances round the bottom, and were covered with heavy white quilts. The bed-ends were brass, except that my grandmother and grand-father slept in a wooden four-poster. It had curtains all round it, but they were never drawn except when children wanted to hide. There was no bathroom, so every bedroom had a marble-topped washstand with a basin, ewer, soap dish and slop-bucket in matching pottery, often with pretty floral designs. A chamber pot of the same pattern was under the bed, and it was emptied each morning, with the washing water, into the slop-bucket. In winter the water in the ewer sometimes froze during the night.

The three earth-closets were outside the house. The first was for the grown-up members of the family, the second was for the children and the maid and the third was for the labourers. The family privies were all set about with fragrant shrubs—syringa, lilac and honeysuckle—and the children's had a long seat with two holes, which enabled them to sit in pairs as they relieved themselves and chat. Each hole had its well-fitting wooden lid and the privies were emptied regularly by a labourer on to a great heap in the orchard called the dung hill. No care nor shrub, however, could palliate the smell of an earth-closet. Therefore in all else they were clean and wholesome to exaggeration. The walls shone brighter with limewash than the cream dairy. The top of the kitchen table was not scrubbed so white as the wood of the privy seats, nor did the bricks of the pantry floor gleam so red as in the closets. Even the lavatory paper, the *Lindsey Star*, reflected this passion to give a good impression in adverse circumstances. The maid was obliged

46

first to iron the sheets of the newspaper flat, and then to cut them with a sharp knife and a ruler into exact squares a quarter of an inch smaller all round than the open wooden boxes in which they were kept at hand.

In a loft over the granary, grandfather bred blue rock pigeons to sell at fourteen shillings a dozen for pigeon shooting. At the shoot, a bird was released from a trap after the attendant had spat into one of its eyes with a spittle of tobacco juice to make it swerve in flight. Only blue rock pigeons were good enough for the Lincolnshire marksmen, so grandfather killed off any that were born brown or white, and they made a delicate meal for the sick. To be really tender they had to be 'squeakers', taken young while their beaks were still soft. Matilda had one of her pet cats shot by grandfather for killing pigeons. Summary justice was meted out to anything that transgressed. For instance, Mary had a favourite hen which was in the habit of laying its eggs on top of the stack and of eating the corn at leisure while up there. One day the hen was up to its tricks, and the maid, knowing what would happen if it was discovered, climbed on the stack to try to dislodge it. However, grandfather saw the hen too soon and fetched his gun and shot it, almost between the maid's legs. It was bad enough when grandfather slaughtered the children's pets himself, but worse when he insisted on delegating the job to them. John had a lurcher called 'Wop', who was a cross between a greyhound and a retriever, a dog bred for poaching. The greyhound in him could run down a hare, and the retriever in him brought it back to his master. Before long there were complaints about his depredations, so grandfather sold him to some gipsies who took him away with them to Louth, about twenty miles away; but as soon as Wop could get free from his new owners he made his way back home to Hedingham. The joyful reunion with his beloved John was intense but short-lived, because this time grandfather made sure that he would be rid of him. He ordered the boys to hang him, and they had to obey, remembering for the rest of their lives this example beyond all others of their father's cruelty.

47

My grandfather and Thomas Millson began farming at
the Glebe inexperienced, under-capitalized, under-stocked,
and in the middle of a long agricultural depression. Before
they started to spend their capital they had two carts, a
harrow, a plough, a drill and a few other implements, all
very old and much repaired. The livestock was three cows
with one calf between them, two horses, and no sheep. One
of the horses had fever in its feet and had to be shod with
oval shoes and the other, Prince, was a 'shiverer', with a
nervous complaint in his back and was liable to bolt. The
land was poor. There were no nettles, those insatiable deep-
rooted lovers of rich sub-soil and graveyards, and the fields
were so full of stones that the children were sent out to pick
them up and pile them beneath the hedges to enable the
land to be worked. Without child labour the partnership
could not have survived. John and James left school as soon
as they were thirteen to work on the farm and the younger
boys laboured in the fields before and after school. There
was no pay, and no thanks. Grandfather complained endlessly of their incompetence, and they could never work

48

hard enough to avoid being thrashed from time to time for idleness. Illness or injuries brought no sympathy. Once when grandfather and Henry were loading hay, he stuck the prong of a hayfork through the flesh between Henry's finger and thumb. Without a word of regret he threw over his great red-spotted handkerchief and said, 'Wrap it up, boy, and get on with your work.' It was the same when James was cutting beet and sliced his finger to the bone. As for George, grandfather mocked him as 'a little hunchbacked dwarf—a disgrace to the farm', a reflection on his stature that was grossly and characteristically unfair. But George was unperturbed and indomitable, and if he was so minded he would dawdle over fetching the cows home with my mother. They had happy times together driving the cattle through rutted old country lanes, chanting 'Cush, cow! Come on! Cush! Cush!' with the smell of greenery all round. There were hedge-tips for the children to nibble, carrots to be pulled up, swedes to gnaw, birds' nests to find, and ponds to visit in the corners of meadows. Always there was something to munch in the fields and hedgerows. If they were too long on the way back to the cowsheds, George would get a thrashing, but he didn't care. He was a bold pugnacious little lad, always ready to chelp his father and, to old Thomas Millson's delight, 'blood up to the eyes'. One day he was whistling and grandfather thrashed him. George still whistled and was thrashed again. Still defiant he continued to whistle, and was once more beaten and was once more unsubdued. As grandfather was about to hit him for the fourth time one of the farm labourers intervened and said, 'If you touch him again, I'll run this fork through you!' And that ended the affair in George's and the farm labourer's favour.

Grandfather constantly urged his family to greater effort by saying, 'We're breaking! Breaking like sticks!' It was an exaggeration, but not a very great one because times were truly hard for farmers. The partners never did in fact break, for there was always Aunt Kate in America to come to the rescue with a loan, but grandfather saw to it

49

that his family lived under the shadow of a bankruptcy that was near enough, though not quite so near as he made out. It helped to keep their minds concentrated on the need for work, and for economy. The family often had no Sunday joint, and even when beef was provided it was brisket, the cheapest. They practically never ate mutton. Their regular meat was pork, and even then the children had to eat the pudding first to dull their appetites. The rule was, 'No pudding—no meat.' Grandfather, of course, kept his own pigs, and when a pig had been killed and dismembered, the bacon was salted in wooden brine troughs. Sometimes it had gone off a little before it reached the table, but grandfather would insist on there being no waste. It had to be eaten. 'There's nothing worse,' Henry once told me, 'than eating bacon that is not quite right.' To cure the hams grandmother rubbed them well with salt. Then she covered them with saltpetre, brown sugar and more salt. Next she coated them with good clean whitewash and smothered them with pepper. That was to keep the flies away and to save the meat from being blown. Then the hams were put in muslin bags and hung from hooks in the kitchen ceiling.

A pig was killed by hoisting it up by the hind legs to a tall tripod of stout poles and it hung there with squeals that were terrible to hear until its throat was cut. Pigs were executed, like St Peter, upside down, with the object of draining the carcass of blood so that the hams and bacon would preserve better. It also facilitated the collection of the blood in a bucket to make black puddings. The perishable parts of a pig could not all be eaten by one family while they were still fresh, so by arrangement between a group of friends and relatives, each killed a pig at different times in the year and distributed the surplus meat amongst the others in the form of pig cheer, which included sausages, pork pies, mince pies, haslets, brawns, a fry and scraps. In fact, pig cheer contained something of almost everything that could be made from the pig, and there was very little of a pig that was not eaten in one form or another. 'Everything,' they used to say, 'but the squeal.' Scraps were pieces of fat that were delicious when fried. Mince pies were included in pig cheer because the pastry was made with the special lard obtained from the leaf-fat of the pig, and the mincemeat itself contained a small amount of minced lungs, or lights. But of all the things my grandmother made from a pig, the most delicious was a stuffed chine. It was a cut, similar to a saddle of mutton, out of the centre of the back of the pig, where the best pork in the whole animal was to be found. The block of raw pork was well rubbed with salt and a smaller quantity of saltpetre. It stood for about a month for the salt to soak in. Then it was hung for several weeks, and when dry the top of the chine was cut in rows so that the deep clefts made by the knife could be stuffed with a finely chopped filling of parsley, marjoram, thyme, chives and blackcurrant leaves. My mother remembered being sent out into the garden for the indispensable three blackcurrant leaves, no more, no less. The furrows in the chine made it look as if ploughed, and the herbs were pressed deep into the incisions so that the greenery showed in lines like a field sprouting a dark green crop in spring. The chine was then baked in a flour paste that was afterwards broken off and thrown away. Stuffed chine was always eaten cold, and usually with old-fashioned salad. Grandmother cut lettuce leaves fairly small, and added chopped spring onions, sugar, salt and pepper. Then the whole was soaked in vinegar for at least an hour, and when eaten with cold pork and cold boiled potatoes the sharp tang of the raw onions and the bitter-sweetness of the vinegar and sugar made an excellent foil to the fatness of the meat and the blandness of the potatoes.

The housekeeping arrangements were that grandfather himself bought in Brigg what little mutton and beef the family ate, so that he could make sure that the cut was a cheap one. He also bought flour by the sack. For the rest of the family's requirements my grandmother had to make do with the egg and butter money. Like other farmers' wives, she kept twenty or thirty chickens which wandered freely in the stackyard and around the farm buildings in the care of a strong white rooster with a large scarlet comb and wattles. Grandfather bought the meal and provided the corn for these birds, but grandmother sold the eggs for housekeeping money. The children fed them with mash before going to school, and in the afternoon they threw them a few handfuls of corn. For the rest of the day the chickens searched the farmyard for food, sometimes halting on one leg to look round and listen for signs of danger, sometimes turning their heads parallel to the ground as if to enable one eye to obtain a better view of what might be lying there; but always on the look-out for anything edible —perhaps a delicious maggot to enrich their eggs, or a flake of grit to harden the shells. They particularly loved to peck about in the rich manure in the crewyard. Grandmother could have supplemented her egg-money income by preparing poultry for sale as table birds, but this she refused to do, to my grandfather's great resentment, because it would have involved plucking off the feathers, and drawing out the intestines, heart, liver and other entrails through an incision in the bird's behind.

The butter money was a much more attractive source of income. Grandfather provided the milk from his cows, and grandmother made the cream into butter with the help of the maid to wind the churn. Then she patted the butter into neat little rectangular blocks with wooden paddles called her 'butter hands' and sold about twenty pounds of it a week at a wholesale price of one shilling and twopence a pound. So the family ate margarine. Grandfather took some of the butter weekly to the butter market under the Town Hall in Brigg, and accounted to her for the proceeds; but the bulk of it was sold by Mr Reade, a shopkeeper in Kirton Lindsey. Grandmother had a roller to run over her pats of butter to mark them with 'Fisher' and a wheatear, which was her trademark, to distinguish her own product from the inferior ones that Mr Reade would otherwise have passed off as hers. Out of the egg and butter money, grandmother could occasionally squeeze a penny or two for the older boys who would otherwise have worked on the farm for nothing.

From the same fund she had to pay for the maid, and grandfather made no contribution for the pleasure he took with her. Grandmother negotiated with a servant girl's mother over a glass of home-made elderberry, damson or cowslip wine, and the price of hiring the daughter was around one shilling and sixpence a week. The first maid was Ruth Pennyman, but within a few months the master had made her pregnant and she had to go. From then on the Fishers had seven different maids in six years, including Selina Kemp, Lucy Nathcoats, Nancy Bingham, Harriet Hare and Moggs Merryweather. They were all obliged to leave, whether by my grandmother's resentment, or by a surfeit of unwelcome advances, or by the consequences of too many well-received attentions. As my Aunt Matilda said, 'If it wasn't father, it was one of the boys.' She omitted to mention old Thomas Millson, but, according to Uncle James, he had neither outlived his sexual desires nor his capacity to gratify them. The best-remembered of the servant girls was Moggs Merryweather, who came to the Glebe when she was fifteen from a poor family in Snitterby. She was not very clean, but she had a fine complexion and deep violet eyes 'set with a smutty finger in a pretty face'. Moggs had a tall graceful figure, and it is not difficult to imagine the importunities a girl so attractive would face in a household with an incontinent master, a pair of adolescent sons, and their still rampant old grandfather. Why she left I never heard, nor whether retribution in the form of maintenance payments ever followed for the little bastard Fishers begotten on the unfortunate serving-girls. There were tales of red-headed children running about the village with my grandfather's features, but silence about who fed them.

The reputation of the Glebe became such that the local mothers would no longer expose their daughters to the hazards of Fisher employment, and eventually grandmother had to find her maids at the annual hiring of servants in Brigg on the Friday before Old May Day. The servant girls who had no work, or who wanted a change of post, used to walk up and down the main street of Brigg on the hiring day.

53

Anyone who required a maid looked them over like fillies in a horse fair and picked out the one who seemed most likely. The farm labourers also offered themselves in the human market on the same Friday. It was known as 'Status Day' from the medieval Statutes of Labourers that had been enacted to keep down the wages of farm workers when they were in short supply after the Black Death. The men dressed in their best blue or green Status suits, which were brightly coloured to attract attention. They wore caps with the peak over one ear, and carried favours in their buttonholes, such as ribbons or celluloid flowers. A lock of hair was wetted and smoothed over the forehead, and thus arrayed they strolled up and down the High Street, looking out for the farmers and leering at the girls. When chosen, a labourer was given a shilling, known as a 'fasten-penny' as an earnest of a year's employment. Then, like a taxi, he altered his appearance to show that he was engaged by wearing his favours in a different way. On the agreed day he would infallibly turn up for work, just as the farmer would certainly accept him on the strength of the bargain sealed by the fasten-penny. The rate of pay was twenty pounds a year, with lodging and keep provided. For non-resident labour, the wages were thirty pounds a year.

As he became established, grandfather needed two labourers—a yardman and a waggoner, or horseman. The waggoner's duties were primarily to look after the horses, and to plough, seed and harrow, but he would turn his hand to hoeing or anything else that was required. The yardman was a general factotum, though mainly responsible for the cows and pigs. The two labourers fed in the kitchen at times different from the children, and both of them slept in one bed in the attic room that had an exclusive staircase from the kitchen. In this way they were effectively segregated from the family. They only went into the kitchen for meals, and through it on their way to and from bed. They washed in an out-house where there was an enamel bowl which they filled from a pump in the yard and emptied down an outside drain. Grandmother provided soap and a roller towel on the back of the out-house door, but no hot water and the men never asked for it, even in mid-winter. A third earth-closet was set aside for them so that they should never use either of the two family ones. The labourers rose at five o'clock and went down into the kitchen to light a fire and to make tea. For breakfast they ate cold fat boiled bacon and bread. For lunch, bacon was wedged between two thick slices of bread, to be eaten out in the fields at eleven o'clock, with cold tea, without milk and sugar, brought in an old whisky bottle. They also had a large jam pasty, hard and brownish, and very inferior to the white ones eaten by the family; but even so, my grandmother's pastry was a recognized inducement to men to work for her husband. Beer was provided only at hay harvest and threshing time. At harvest they drank it at the eleven o'clock break, or in the evening when they were stacking. Also, great cans of hot tea were taken out into the fields by the maid, or by the children, as well as baskets full of apple cakes. They were large apple pies baked in soup plates and, as a special harvest treat, made of good flour.

At threshing time, grandfather hired machinery from a contractor, and the steam traction engine panted into the stack-yard, towing the threshing machine. Then the engine and the thresher were stationed a belt's length apart, and securely chocked to hold them in place. Next, the traction engine was put out of gear so that it could run as a stationary engine to supply power from its fly-wheel to the thresher by means of a long, wide, and surprisingly slack belt which crossed over itself between the two machines in a figure of eight. Henry remained captivated all his life by traction engines. They displayed their charms for all to see, high above the boiler, and a child could stand for hours fascinated as the long lazy swinging belt carried energy to the thresher. The piston drove to and fro in so leisurely a fashion that every surge of power could be observed. The flywheel was in no hurry either, utterly confident of its own momentum. But the most compelling sight was the governor. Its two iron balls span round above the rest of the works, contemptuously alone, and at right angles to everything else. The governor seemed an irrelevance, or mere extravagance of movement, yet it was the controlling brain. If the engine speed increased, the balls swung higher and closed the steam-cock; and as they fell they opened the valve again. The thresher, however, was less interesting, because there was little to see. All was enclosed in a wooden casing, but for the long conveyor arm which contained a rotating belt of sharp prongs. The men loaded sheaves of long-stemmed wheat, barley or rye into the thresher, from which they emerged as straw at one point, as chaff at another, and as a torrent of grain to be caught in sacks at the third.

When threshing, my grandfather was on tenterhooks to see that the break for lunch, when beer, bread and cheese were brought out, was as short as possible because every moment the machinery stayed in the yard was money spent, and every moment the men rested was money wasted. The contractor's foreman did not tell the master when he thought it was time to break off, but he gave a sign to the engineman, who slowly closed the valve. The pulsing of the piston grew slower, and that was the first indication grandfather had that they were about to stop. Immediately he rushed over to the house crying, 'They're stopping! They're stopping!' The beer and cheese had to be out instantly, or there was trouble. Once it had been served he hovered about uneasily, lest the men should eat and drink too slowly. But nothing could be done until the engineman, in his own good time, had climbed back into his metal seat and turned the steam-cock and filled the cylinder with the scalding steam that had previously hissed furiously out of the safety-valve with an impatience only equalled by my grandfather's. The thresher poured out the chaff on to a large sheet spread on the ground, and grandfather hired a huge half-witted lad called Billie Patchett to carry it away. He was so strong that he could gather up the corners of the sheet unaided and sling it over his shoulder. He was notorious for an insatiable appetite, so when there was to be a Harvest Tea at the Chapel, some-one gave Billie sixpence to go and eat as much as he could.

He arrived early, and when he saw the food for the village spread out on the tables—pork pies, ham sandwiches, cakes in their hundreds—he burst into tears and cried, 'I can't eat all that!'

An ordinary working day for the labourers at the Glebe began when they went out into the fields at six. They had their lunch at eleven and the yardman came in at one o'clock for dinner, whereas the waggoner went on with his ploughing or other work until two o'clock when the horses were brought in, having completed their yoke. For the men's dinners, the maid set aside hot fat bacon, potatoes and pudding from the family dinner. From two o'clock till six the yardman went on with his afternoon work, such as cleaning out the cowsheds or crewyard; and the waggoner, having put away his horses to rest, did odd jobs from three o'clock to six, which was time for supper. Needless to say, supper consisted of cold fat bacon, bread and tea. In fact the men consumed little meat other than pork, and it was part of the hiring bargain that each was entitled to a pig a year. After supper the men could go to a public house, so long as it was not the one frequented by the farmers; but even in winter they were not allowed into the house, so they never sat by a fireside. The only warmth they had was from the horses in the stable and the hay in the cut-house, which was their winter recreation room. Servants from other families could join them there, and they played cards and dominoes on the top of the corn-bin by the light of a paraffin storm-lantern. At nine o'clock it was time for bed and they went silently through the kitchen and up the back staircase to their room. Such was a farm-labourer's day, and there were no holidays and no days off, except that on Sunday work was limited to essential services to the livestock. Consequently, of all the days of the week, Sunday was the day on which my grandfather was the most irritable.

During the long working week-days, the labourers were expected to be busy all the time. If grandfather found one of his men scything, for example, and in his opinion idling, he would seize the implement, saying, 'Give that to me! I'll show you how to scythe !' Then he would work feverishly for several minutes, till he threw down the scythe and went off home with a parting shot : 'There ! That's how to do it !' On reaching the house he lay on the couch and had palpitations, calling weakly for his wife to bring a tot of brandy. Apart from these brief and exhausting demonstrations, grandfather only did manual work at seed-time and harvest. On Thursdays, without fail, he went to the corn market in Brigg and in accordance with the old saying that the eye of the master is worth both his hands, he spent the other days of the week supervising and criticizing the work of his two labouring sons and his two labouring men. Predictably, none of the hired labourers liked my grandfather. Nor did he like them—with one strange and unaccountable exception which the family could never understand because he was most certainly attracted by women. Even so, there was one yokel about whom my mother said he was 'perfectly silly'. She told me that he once refused to eat a particularly delicious dinner unless his favourite could share it. My grandmother, who had been a domestic servant, was outraged : 'Masters don't treat men like that !'

On summer evenings, if the labourers did not go to the public houses, they spent their time out in the fields fornicating with the village girls or congregating at stiles to watch the farmers' daughters, noses up-tilted, climb over them to the accompaniment of their lewd commentary. Farmers' daughters did not consort with labourers. My mother retained the greatest scorn for them : 'A poor silly lot !' But she remembered two of her father's men more kindly, 'Lovely Gilbert from Yorkshire, and one handsome young rake with divine blue eyes'. Matilda had more than scorn for farm labourers, and for a good reason that arose out of her fondness for solitude. She spent as much time as she could alone in quiet corners of the farm buildings absorbed in romantic but edifying novels, particularly by Mrs Henry Wood. Her retreat was also partly calculated to keep her out of sight when there was work to be done, because she was always given the rough jobs. However, that practice incited Josh Partridge, the waggoner, to way-lay her with evil intentions in an outhouse when she was fourteen. Fortunately young Matilda was wearing one of the large straw hats of those days, plentifully decorated, that needed a long sharp hat-pin to keep it in place. Disengaging one of her arms from the enforced embrace, she reached up to her hat and plucked out the great pin. At this the waggoner did not take alarm. He was foolish enough to think that Matilda was beginning to co-operate by removing at least her hat, but he was speedily disabused when she plunged the pin with all her strength into his buttocks. The stout corduroy trousers absorbed some of the impact, but not enough to preserve Josh from a penetration that was deep enough to leave the pin embedded like Excalibur in the stone. He gave a roar of pain and clapped both hands to his behind, thus releasing his victim who immediately made her escape, clutching her now unsecured hat to her head as she went. The waggoner suffered no further retribution because Matilda told no one of her experience. She felt shamed and contaminated to have been the object of a labourer's lust, and it was abhorrent that even her mother should know of it. In consequence Matilda had to endure the continued presence of Josh about the farm until he left at the end of his year's contract; but he made no further attacks upon her. 'After I'd driven it home a couple of inches,' said Matilda years later, 'even Josh Partridge took the point that his advances were unwelcome.'

For the children at the Glebe there were no manufactured playthings, no model railways, clockwork toys, scooters, bicycles, tennis racquets, footballs. The only dolls the girls ever had were made of old pieces of cloth, stuffed with sawdust, with shirt buttons for eyes, wool for hair, and two rows of red stitches for a mouth. There were no birthday presents, and at Christmas the gifts were minimal. Each young child had an old long woollen stocking hung at the bedhead. It was always packed to the same pattern: an apple in the toe, then nuts and either a sugar pig or sugar mouse with a few wrapped sweets and chocolates in the foot of the stocking.

An orange filled the heel, and in the leg they found such small and inexpensive presents as a bright new penny, a handkerchief, a pencil and exercise book, a comb, wrapped dates and figs. There was no Christmas tree, but after the children had gone to bed on Christmas Eve, grandmother hung a 'mistletoe bough' over the living-room door. There was no mistletoe in it. It was a rough ball of evergreens with Christmas decorations stuck in amongst the leaves. The decorations were very splendid because Aunt Kate had sent them from America. The place of honour at the top of the bough was always taken by a silver fairy sitting on a crescent moon. As the children came in to breakfast on Christmas morning, the custom was for grandfather and grandmother to stand under the mistletoe bough and to kiss each child as he came in. Christmas dinner consisted of a large joint of roast beef because for the rest of the year, if they had beef at all, it was brisket. After the beef came a Christmas pudding, boiled in a cloth, with a sprig of holly in the top, and eaten with a white sauce laced with whisky.

For the remainder of the year the Fisher children had no presents and no pocket-money even to buy sweets. This was largely due to there being, with a large family to be clothed and fed, no money to spare; but it was also partly due to their father's meanness. When my grandmother was a child in Redbourne she had been more fortunate. Her father gave her a penny now and then, and she used to spend it on boiled sweets in the shape of fishes. She and the two cats would sit on the doorstep of the blacksmith's house taking licks in turn but my grandmother lived, nevertheless, to be ninety-three. However, until Aunt Kate started to visit the Glebe from America, the only time the Fishers had a sweet was once a week on bath night, when Aunt Hiles, the family midwife who had ushered them all into the world, used to visit them on Saturday evenings to see them naked again in a zinc tub set in front of the kitchen fire. To soften the rigour of the occasion she bought each of them a sweet. This benefactress was born Elizabeth Maitland, but when she married Joseph Hiles her Christian name fell into disuse. He remained Uncle Joseph, while she, as was customary, became Aunt Hiles to make clear that she was now an appendage of her husband. Joseph was extremely unctuous and self-righteous. His wife was afraid of thunder and would hide her head under the bed-clothes, but she had little comfort from him : 'If you're afraid of this little sign of God's wrath, what will you be like on Judgment Day?' Uncle Joseph taught in the chapel Sunday school, admonishing the children, 'Now, now, my little sinners ! If you can't behave I shall have to use the rod !' It was no idle threat, because at Sunday school Anglican and Nonconformist children were as freely beaten, boys and girls alike, as Roman Catholics were assaulted in their institutions, and with similar gratification to their instructors.

In the absence of pocket money and presents, everything the children played with was made in the village. An Atkinson uncle, for they were all joiners, would turn them a top on his lathe, and anyone could make a whip with a stick and an old leather boot-lace. The blacksmith's shop provided the children with iron bowling hoops, and the infamous Josh Partridge made powerful catapults for them with the fork of a hazel branch, the leather tongue of an old boot, and thick square elastic bought by the yard in Kirton and bound with waxed thread. Grandfather would pay for catapult elastic because the boys shot the blackbirds which ate the fruit. 'By God !' my Uncle George told me. 'We knew how to use a catterpelt. I was a demon with one !' The blacksmith's shop had also filled a cupboard at the Glebe with old skates which could be fastened by straps on to an ordinary pair of boots. So when the ponds were frozen hard all the children went out on to the ice. It was exceptional for my grandfather to cater in the least degree for any useless pastime but he happened to like skating himself. When the ice was suitable he would join his family on the largest pond in the village and woe betide any who got in his way. The skates were designed for speed, with long blades sharpened like knives and extending far beyond the toes and heels of the boot, with an upward curl at the front like the prow of a ship. The blades were set in blocks of wood with slots in them for the straps to pass through, and they were made very long so that when a foot was turned sideways to the direction of travel a powerful purchase could be obtained by biting the keen edge into the ice along its whole length. It was a fine sight to see grandfather, wearing an old woollen cap with a bobble on the top, his tall thin figure leaning forwards, bent almost double, his legs thrashing and throwing up splinters of ice, careering madly round the perimeter of the pond with his arms contemptuously folded behind his back. At those moments his children felt almost an affection for him, as they did when he revealed another human weakness for cricket. Sometimes he played in the village team, and used his strong blacksmith's arms to clout ball after ball clean beyond the edges of the Green until he missed one of the few going straight for the wicket. When he bowled, it was in a whirlwind of passionate desire to see the stumps fly. Grandfather could do nothing, whether at work or at play, unless it was done at high speed and with a great expenditure of energy. If he ever tried to milk a cow, the beast would simply decline to let her milk down in response to his impatient tuggings and squeezings. Then he would curse her for her brute obstinacy, kick the pail from under her belly, and go find a woman to do the job for him.

In spite of the rudimentary equipment for play, a child's life at the Glebe was often intensely happy. My mother said that her childhood had 'the glory and freshness of a dream'. On all my aunts and uncles Hedingham made so deep an impression that they were never tired of going back in their tracks and shedding fifty or sixty years to live again in the small, turbulent, vivid community they had created for themselves. Much of the work they had to do may have been drudgery—hoeing beet, scrubbing the cobbled corsey with a yard-broom, cleaning out the stable, weeding the garden, pumping water from the well, mending socks, chopping sticks—but some was enjoyable. There were sick lambs to be fed with a bottle, blackbirds' nests to be found and destroyed, cows and sheep to be driven, mangolds to be shredded with the rotary cutter, the cowshed to be whitewashed. When there was time for leisure, the whole countryside was open to them. Out of doors the children were, according to Matilda, 'as wild as wind'. Even John, with his weak heart, ran and leapt about like the rest of them. They bathed naked in the streams, boys and girls together; they fished for gudgeon and an occasional roach with a stick and bent pin on the end of a length of thread. They knew where the best frogs' spawn was to be found, and the best trees for climbing. The ponds were navigable in a large brine trough. If there were any laws against bird-nesting, they made no difference. The boys knew the birds of the north Lincolnshire air, not only by their cries and songs, but by their eggs and nests : the marvellously neat and industrious wren, the almost undiscoverable skylark, the inaccessible woodpecker, and the dangerous swan which, they believed, could peck out an eye or break a leg with a flap of its wing. And there were games to be played more hazardous than raiding swans' nests. Bulls were kept unchained in the fields, and Uncle Robert Anderson had a particularly savage red shorthorn, with wicked bloodshot eyes. The boys loved to tease it from the edge of the en-closure by waving their red spotted handkerchiefs until it charged. Then they ran to the five-barred gate and climbed over before the beast could get at them. The gate was rein-forced by a very heavy pole slung across on chains, and this eventually gave Henry an idea. The boys stood the pole on end and opened the gate. He waited by the pole and the others goaded the bull to charge them. As it was thundering head down, through the gateway, Henry dropped the pole neatly on to its skull and the bull was felled to the ground for several minutes. Then it staggered to its feet and wan-dered rather aimlessly back into the field, considerably chastened. Robert Anderson was well enough aware of the young Fishers' love of bull-baiting to ask them why his beast was looking so dazed and dispirited. The only expla-nation Henry could offer was that it must have had a stroke.

Activities of that kind were pursued at the risk of a

thrashing, if not of their lives, but the boys were encouraged to take their catapults out into the woodlands to shoot rabbits because they ate the crops and could themselves be eaten in a pie as a welcome change from fat boiled bacon. Effective rabbit-catching needed ferrets, which were carried in the inner pockets of the boys' jackets. Once when Henry was looking into his inside pocket for his ferret, the animal sprang up and bit his lip and clung on, sucking blood, until one of his brothers was able to choke it. Nothing else would induce a ferret to let go. One day Robert thought it a good jest to ask my innocent mother to take a ferret out of a bag for him, and of course it had hold of her finger in a flash. Nevertheless, squirrels were held in even greater respect for their teeth. 'Squirrills,' my Uncle George told me, 'have a wickid bite!' And they were red squirrels, not the more formidable grey. Not only were the boys encouraged to catch rabbits, but in winter, when the hedges were bare of leaves, blackbirds were hunted to reduce their numbers before the mating season. The method was for two boys to walk slowly along a hedge, one on each side and both advancing at the same pace. This tended to deter the birds from flying out until within range of a catapult. At one time grandfather encouraged the boys to shoot thrushes as well as blackbirds, but grandmother, who loved them for their song, taught him to be more discriminating. She asked her sons to catch a thrush alive and he was put in a cage by the back door. Then grandmother offered him corn, fruit, bread, meat and other things to eat; but while the bird accepted a varied diet he would never touch the fruit, and so saved the lives of many of his kind.

Larks were shot for food, not for their tongues but for their breasts, which were cut out and baked in a pie. In those days there were thousands of them in the fields—so many that the little children who could not shoot were sent out amongst the crops with clappers merely to 'tent larks', to frighten them away. They noticed that a lark is unusual in having a spur on its feet pointing to the rear, so in my family anyone with large heels is called 'lark heeled'. Sparrows, too, were hunted for food, and in the words of my Uncle George, 'A sparrer's a lovely little breast!' The boys also shot, or snared, moorhens, plovers and ducks, though the moorhens had a muddy taste from feeding on the bottom of ponds. Rooks perched too high in the tops of tall trees for the boys to reach them with catapults, but when they were older grandfather provided a muzzle-loading flintlock that he bought for a shilling at a sale. Then those flea-ridden creatures were brought home, and it was Matilda's task to skin them and to cut off their legs and breasts for cooking in a huge pie. 'Lousy damn things!' said Matilda. The trouble with rook pie was that, when cooked, the pieces of meat inside were so bright pink that the girls were reminded of the flesh of little babies and were unable to eat any.

The gun was loaded by ramming in the powder first, then wadding, then the shot, and finally more wadding to hold the charge in. Once loaded, the gun could only be unloaded by firing it. So my grandmother said repeatedly that if the boys failed to find anything to shoot, the gun must be fired into the air before being brought back into the house where it was hung on hooks in the ceiling of the living-room—but to save powder and shot it never was. One day Matilda was sitting at the table in the living-room drawing plovers—'nasty dark-skinned brutes'—when Robert came in with the gun still loaded and made to hang it across the hooks in the beam in the ceiling. He happened to catch the trigger in his coat button and the gun went off. The shots ricocheted off the wall and some of the pellets hit Matilda in the back of the hand. Most of them came out again through the broken skin, but one remained for a long time until grandfather gave her a penny to let him cut it out with his sharp penknife.

Matilda was always shocked when her brothers brought pheasants and partridges home to be plucked and drawn, because they were reserved as game for the gentry, but in practice game was poached in and out of season by any method that was silent and inconspicuous. The birds were lured into a convenient field by scattering corn there for several days. Then from the cover of the hedge they could sometimes be knocked over with a catapult as they fed. If not, there was a more sophisticated way of catching them. Creed corn was threaded on horsehair with a needle, and thrown out on to the field. Partridges would gobble it, horsehair and all, but once down their necks, the threaded corn stuck in their gullets and the birds, catching for breath, staggered about unable to take off. So the boys rushed out from the hedge, caught them alive, and wrung their choking necks. Pheasants could be taken in the same way, but with raisins threaded on cotton. The Fishers ate their game fresh. It was plucked, drawn and into the oven as quickly as possible for reasons both prudent and gastronomic. Those who were obliged to eat home-cured bacon did not choose to eat rotting pheasants. The prudence was more out of respect for the law than fear of its sanctions. Henry was once caught by the gamekeeper of the local hunt, which also enjoyed the shooting rights. The master was all prepared to have him hauled up before the magistrates, where poachers had as sympathetic a hearing as blasphemers before an archdeacon. When Robert Anderson heard that Henry was to be prosecuted he called on the master of the hunt and told him that if his nephew was taken to court no member of the hunt would thenceforth 'set hoof' anywhere within his three hundred acres. So Henry was not prosecuted for poaching but well thrashed for being caught.

The three girls, Mary, Matilda and my mother, spent their leisure in more lawful pursuits. They searched the meadows, streams and woodlands for wild flowers. They knew where in the woods to find the drifts of aconites, anemones and bluebells. They roamed the fields and hedgerows looking for the rarer speedwells, sweet violets, wild pansies, scarlet pimpernels—anything that was small and delicate and retiring. There was a profusion of wild flowers everywhere. Poppies, thistles and cornflowers flourished unsprayed amongst the wheat; daisies and buttercups usurped the meadows; and the streams were cluttered with yellow kingcups and tall bulrushes like long brown pokers.

My mother found 'wonderful treasures' in the fields—yellow heartsease, lady's fingers, pennyroyal, Venus's looking-glass, and mother of thousands. Once she came across a clump of magenta ragged robins so gaudy and abandoned in their brilliance that they brought, she said, 'all Heaven before my eyes'. The air seemed intensely still, though there was the sound of children shouting, a dog barking, perhaps a very distant train on the Kirton line, and above all the music of the skylarks straining and fluttering upwards and then dropping earthwards like a stone. One of her father's fields sloped down in one corner to a pond with a large ash tree shading it. By the roots of the tree, a little ledge ran above the water and was overgrown with long grass and straggling shoots from the hedge-bottom. Here my mother used to burrow in amongst the greenery and perch herself precariously over the pond. All was quiet and sunshine pierced the foliage in strange patterns. There were curious little flowers and growths, such as pear-grey fungus that looked like tiny wine glasses, and sometimes a few white anemones, and always interesting spiders and insects. This was my mother's own private world. Looking down into the pool she was a water-nymph, and across her reflected face strange creatures skated with long hair-like legs.

Thomas Millson had some experience of farming because as a village blacksmith he was also a small holder and had usually taken the prize given by the Duke of St Albans for the best cottager's cow. His fondness for the brute creation, however, made him quite unfitted for serious agriculture. When the weather was cold, he hated to take the cart-horses out of the stable; and when it was hot, he could not bear to see them sweating in the fields. Not the least of my grandfather's difficulties was to keep his partner from overfeeding the stock. One day he was at his favourite occupation of tipping turnips into a feeding-trough when a ram attacked him from behind and butted him clean over it. The animal persisted in his assault and Thomas only stopped him by cracking his skull with an iron bar. In spite of this demonstration of animal ingratitude, Thomas continued to overfeed every creature he could. His beasts never strayed because he 'tethered them by the mouth'—they couldn't eat anywhere better than at home. As for the pigs, he was not allowed to feed them at all and was discouraged from feeding anything else. There was not much other work that a man over seventy could do on the farm, so Thomas's role in the partnership soon became limited to being the major contributor of capital. With that he was very content because his life in retirement was so agreeable. According to Matilda he had 'the time of his life, the old humbug!' He rose for breakfast on the stroke of nine by his own tall clock on the landing, and grandmother gently brushed his hair and fastened his collar and tie. A freshly laid brown egg was boiled lightly on the fire for exactly three minutes. Newly baked bread was cut wafer-thin and spread with grandmother's own butter. Coffee was made for him when the rest of the family had to be content with tea. A tray was laid with a spotless white cloth. Salt was poured on the side of his plate in a little cone that was then patted down flatter with the back of the salt-spoon so that it would not spill over the plate when the tray was carried to the living-room where Thomas sat alone by the fire and breakfasted. Other rituals attended his going to bed. Precisely at nine in the evening a saucepan of milk, newly milked at six o'clock, was put over a still fire, because a flaming fire might have smoked it. Mary had to watch the milk rise, and old Millson never failed to say, 'Let it *boil*, Maria!' Then the milk was poured over small, exact and equal cubes of home-made bread, well sugared, from which the crusts had been cut. Great-grandfather ate three-quarters of it, and left his spoon in the rest for Fanny, the youngest child and his favourite. He would have left more for her if grandmother's disapproving eye had not been on him.

When Thomas had finished supper, grandmother fetched his slippers and unlaced his boots. A brick had been heating since tea-time in the side-oven. It was wrapped in scorched sheeting, then in blanketing, and was carried upstairs to be put at the foot of his bed. Then Fanny and he went off happily together to their prayers and sleep in the best bed-room. My mother shared a double bed with him until she was eight, but at that point my grandmother decreed that they must part on the grounds that 'his breath was old and hers was young, and their breaths ought not to mingle'.

Nevertheless he continued to nurse her for hours in the elegant old eighteenth-century mahogany rocking-chair he had brought with him from Redbourne. My grandmother remonstrated that Fanny was too heavy, but he replied, 'Nay, Bessie! Don't deprive me of that comfort!' When nursing her, he folded double his large red silk handkerchief with white spots, and spread it on the shoulder of his rough tweed jacket for her head to rest upon. Then she was soon rocked to sleep as the fire crackled and spat and the paraffin lamp hissed and droned. Shortly before her death, my mother wrote of 'my beautiful life' and started it as a small child cuddled up on her grandfather's knee. Thomas took my mother for walks after putting on her little red cape and bonnet trimmed with fur and they went out together into the fields, for the woods were too far away. They had a favourite place by a gate, where there was a stone on which Thomas could sit while Fanny searched about for clumps of tall stiff Canterbury bells and other flowers she particularly loved. Sometimes he would tease her, as he could never resist teasing his favourite animals. He would sit on the fence on the top of a bank, and push her down with the tip of his walking-stick every time she tried to climb towards him saying, 'Why then! The little thing can't help falling down!' Or, 'Bless me, Lovie! Thou can't get up!'

Grandmother made a far greater fuss of her father than she did of her husband, and waited on him hand and foot. Whereas she would wash Thomas's feet, she would never wash my grandfather's. So he used to ask for a similar service from his daughters in a rather deprived and pathetic way. The job was done grudgingly, and that was just as well because grandfather was inordinately fond of having his feet washed, and would have asked for it every night. He folded up his trousers above the knees and put his feet in a white oval porcelain footbath, and let them soak while he sat puffing at his pipe. Then, after one of his daughters had washed and dried his feet, my grandmother might condescend to trim his corns and hard skin with a cut-throat razor. For him she did it with reluctance, but for her

father with the utmost readiness and the favourable treatment Thomas enjoyed at the Glebe bred understandable
resentment in her husband, which showed in occasional
outbursts of temper against him. Then Thomas would go
off to Grays in Essex to stay with his son Tom, but he soon
came back to his daughter's home comforts. Also he hated
to miss Sunday in Hedingham when out came his red leather
prayer book, and Fanny and he went hand in hand to church.
Of the other Fishers only Henry and Matilda were Angli-
cans, Matilda because she liked to worship with the upper
classes, and Henry because he loved one of them. She was
Nancy Pitt-Melville and close to him in age. In everything
else she was very remote, because he only saw her when she
rode through the village attended by her governess and
groom, or when she appeared in the front pew of Hedingham Church, where the congregation sat from east to west
in strict social order—gentry, freehold farmers, tenant
farmers, tradesmen, labourers, domestic servants.

The Pitt-Melvilles lived in a white Regency house hidden
in a small park, almost a mile outside the village, and not
much larger than the biggest of the Andersons' farmhouses.
Thomas Melville, a successful brewer in Newark, had
bought it with fifteen hundred acres of land. His son Roger
now lived there as a gentleman farmer with the adopted
name of Pitt-Melville and a coat of arms. He was busy
establishing himself as an idle country gentleman, Justice
of the Peace, Deputy Lieutenant, Master of Fox Hounds,
and reasonably competent slaughterer of pheasants and
partridges—but there was no touching of forelocks for him.
The only houses he owned were his own, his farm-bailiff's,
and a few labourers' cottages. My relatives would defer to
his fifteen hundred acres, because they deferred to acres, but
he was not their landlord with power to remove the roofs
from over their heads or the land from under their hoes.
So not much regard was paid to the Pitt-Melvilles, except
by Henry who, from his vantage point on the decanal side
of the choir stalls, was well placed to worship their twelve-
year-old daughter—which he did with a characteristic blend

71

of social ambition and erotic longing. It was a very heavy and disturbing mixture taken twice weekly on Sundays to the sound of the English liturgy, and most particularly when the anthem was Martin Peerson's 'Lord ever Brydle my Desires', one of the Rector's favourites. Nancy had long straight yellow hair, a thin face, large cool grey eyes, and slightly protruding teeth. She was not beautiful, but fascinating in her remoteness, in the mystery of what she did at home, what she talked about, what she ate, how many baths a week she had, and what sort of drawers she wore. He ruminated on these and on other more indelicate questions during the Rector's sermons, wondering whether Nancy would in fact behave very differently from his female cousins if he could be alone with her in a hay loft. The black-haired Anderson twins, identical only in their curiosity, had lain with him in secluded places for their mutual edification; and while the Rector was preaching about St Paul's missionary journeys Henry would day-dream of possible destinations for a cool white hand instead of two warm brown ones.

These impertinent speculations about the squire's daughter remained unresolved because Henry only saw her in church, or sometimes riding through the village. He could sing to her, but never speak to her, so he had to make the best of what opportunities he had to command her attention. Fortunately the Rector provided them because he still hankered after the polyphony of King's College Chapel, although the full choir of Hedingham Church was incapable of singing anything more difficult than hymns and psalms. In fact the alto line would have been missing altogether if Mr Smith had not revived a practice of the heyday of English madrigals. Elizabethan and Jacobean domestic servants were hired by musical families for their ability to read and sing a part, so in every cathedral city of England the Rector advertised his willingness to overpay a young groom-gardener if he could sing counter-tenor. The result was that Hedingham Church acquired a very reasonable male alto at the expense of Southwell Minster. Mr Smith himself was a competent tenor and Mr Palfreyman, the schoolmaster on weekdays and church organist on Sundays, could sing bass and read a part with complete reliability. So the Rector had only to find a couple of musical boys in the village to sing the treble line together, or to split when necessary, for him to have a group of five choristers capable of singing the works of Byrd, Tallis, Weekles, Tomkins, Orlando Gibbons and others of that genre. Mr Smith had the good sense to forego masses altogether out of deference to a Protestant village. For the same reason, motets in Latin were only ventured once a quarter, and he denied himself even an anthem in the vernacular more frequently than once a month to save the feelings of the rest of the choir, who were then required to sit mute and inglorious while the expert five demonstrated their superiority. Careful always to avoid unpopularity, Charles Smith paid handsomely for the monthly silence of his incompetent choristers—as he paid generous dowries for the lifelong discretion of his pregnant mistresses. So at Matins on the first Sunday of every month Henry Fisher sang first treble in the small choir, with his cousin Billy Atkinson beside him. The groom-gardener with his hooting falsetto provided the alto line to the unfailing derision of the congregation, who assumed from the pitch of his voice, and correctly, that he was effeminate. The parson moved to the choir stalls to add the tenor part and, since they always sang unaccompanied, the organist left his console to come and sing the bass.

Henry was overjoyed if it was a five-part anthem, with Billy and him going separate ways. Then Nancy could not fail to distinguish his voice, and of all the members of the congregation it was she who seemed most to appreciate and best to understand what counterpoint was about. Her eyes followed the themes as they shifted from one singer to another, and when Henry had the lead they rested on him. If he returned her gaze and even ventured a smile to acknowledge her attention, very occasionally Nancy would shyly return it before quickly dropping her eyes to the prayer book on her knee. In these moments Henry enjoyed for the first time the elation that comes from establishing with a desirable but apparently inaccessible woman that each is pleased that they are aware of each other. Thenceforth it was not entirely ridiculous for him to hope that eventually, somehow or other, he might hold the squire's daughter in his arms. These grounds for hope only increased his longing, and it was particularly acute when the small choir sang Palestrina's 'Sicut Cervus Desiderat ad Fontes Aquarum'. The Rector had translated the Latin for them and, as the hart panteth after the water-brooks, so Henry sang of his desire for Nancy. Billy Atkinson sang in his usual business-like way for his generous choir pay of sixpence a week, and the counter-tenor sang of his need for Billy. The *fontes aquarum* were, for the Rector, release from the flesh, because his was all too well satisfied; whereas the school-master found Palestrina's fuss about his soul panting for the Almighty rather tiresome and excessive, though well done in its way. The village found it as boring as all the Rector's other anthems, which they tolerated as another of the inevitable eccentricities of a rich man who had, unwisely, been sent to college.

Nevertheless, there was a visitor to the Glebe who told me many years later of her delight and astonishment at hearing Palestrina sung in a remote village of North Lincolnshire. She was a half-Greek cousin, Katie Mordell, *née* Polynopoulos, of whom more will be written in its proper place. It must suffice to say now that Cousin Katie, who had studied the piano in Vienna under Paderewski, never forgot 'Sicut Cervus' in Hedingham Church. After the Third Collect for Grace, she saw the Rector move to the choir stalls and, with no preliminary announcement, start to sing the long G on 'Sicut', and almost complete the first two words of the anthem alone. Then came the magical moment when the counterpoint started to develop with the fluting slow entry of the musical groom, a fifth higher, while the Rector broke into crotchets. Next it was for the boys to sound the long hissing sibilant of the opening G an octave higher while the Rector and his groom continued to inter-

74

twine in crotchets and quavers beneath them. Finally the bottom layer of the polyphony was added when the school-master repeated the G, and held it steadily below them all until he, in his turn, was ready to break into crotchets as the original theme became indistinguishable, in the welter of words and sounds, to any but the most discriminating. For all this, the unappreciative village was indebted to the Rector's deep wondering adoration of counterpoint. The greatest aptitude for pleasure he conferred by his example upon my Uncle Henry was, after the pursuit of love, a devotion to polyphony. Henry always maintained that love and counterpoint were complementary, sharing the same simultaneous loss and preservation of identity, and both as subtle and infinitely pleasing as the participants were capable of making them.

My grandmother had no time at all for polyphonic church music, and not much time for love. When listening to singing of any kind her first requirement was that she should hear the words clearly, and the second that they should be in English. So even if she had not been reared in Redbourne, which made her 'sick of parsondom', she would not have been tempted to Hedingham Church by the an-thems. However, she felt that she ought to attend some place of worship, so chapel it had to be, with all its trials. There were, for example, the unmarried farm labourers, about whom she protested endlessly. Their behaviour in chapel was abominable. At first they had been required to sit on forms facing the choirmen near the rostrum where they were under control, but later they had taken it upon them-selves to occupy the back seats of the chapel where my grandmother considered 'they had no business' because all the pews were rented and paid for. From there they provided a chorus to the main drama in the form of a loutish commen-tary, raucous guffaws of laughter, and constant bangs and shufflings. The preachers were another trial, and they almost drove grandmother back into the arms of the church. She would return from evening service cursing the 'duffing preacher', and his 'sad wob' or 'sore drivel'. In fact, little was to be expected of the local preachers who were on 'the Plan'. Every Sunday a local brother, generally unread, unlettered, and often conceited, was sure of a hearing at the morning and evening services. There was Albert Parkinson from Normanby-by-Spital who could hardly read or write but could tell his astonished congregation the number of capital A's in the Bible; and provide other illuminating scriptural statistics. Apart from the satisfaction of an audience that he could never have secured by any other kind of activity, a preacher's reward was a good hot dinner at the house of one of the Hedingham faithful and a decent supper after a second performance at the evening service.

When it was the time for one of the more superior preachers to visit Hedingham on his circuit, my grandmother would give him dinner and some of them were, in my mother's estimation, 'fine interesting men'. She even spoke of 'scholars and thinkers' visiting her home after they had preached in the chapel: but my mother was ever one for turning geese into swans. The chapels, and many churches, provided ready-made audiences for people who could never have commanded listeners to their ideas, nor spectators of their histrionics, in any other walk of life. They provided other opportunities too. Mr Page-Woodcock, of Page-Woodcock's Wind Pills fame, diverted the young girls by turning nursery rhymes into moral stories, with Little Jack Horner and Bo-peep appearing in the role of Wesleyan saints. Mr Page-Woodcock was sixty, grey-haired, tall and handsome—a typical actor-preacher. My mother found his facial contortions 'sweet to see'. Unfortunately, when he gave the little girls rides on his bicycle, he laid his hand upwards on the saddle so that he could tickle them through their knickers. So the virtuous little girls learned to beware of the religious wind-pills manufacturer, and only those in need of salvation went for bicycle rides.

If my grandmother was in a state of constant spiritual unrest under the tribulations of chapel-going, my grandfather had long since lost what little faith he ever had.

Nevertheless, he insisted that his three Anglican children went to church, and that all the others accompanied their mother to chapel. This left the coast clear at home on Sunday evenings for him to enjoy the servant girl in comfort, as his son Robert discovered when, after the family had set out for chapel, he was sent running home to fetch a forgotten hymn-book. All unsuspecting, he burst into the living-room to find his father already half-naked and undressing the maid on the hearth rug in front of a blazing fire. He had a thrashing the next day to teach him more discretion. As long as the family was out of the house on Sunday evenings, my grandfather was indifferent whether they went to church or chapel, though he himself had been brought up a Nonconformist. As an infant he was baptized into the Wesleyan Church, and as an adult if he ever felt the need to attend a place of worship, which was seldom, he went to chapel. For what he called 'hatches, matches and despatches', he was even prepared to undergo an Anglican service; but on Sundays generally he preferred to stay at home and make love to the maid. In contrast, his father, John Fisher, had moved in the opposite direction as recommended, for others, by Voltaire. After a very feckless, and even dissolute, youth and manhood, he had repented under the influence of a revivalist preacher and in old age was attending to his salvation.

John Fisher appeared at the Glebe now and then without warning, like a heavenly messenger, and could be seen kneeling in the middle of the living-room, his elbows resting on the horse-hair sofa, and praying loudly; one moment calling upon the Blessed Redeemer to save his relatives from damnation, and the next moment interrupting his devotions to take swigs from a bottle of whisky on the floor beside him. He had fallen a victim to the religious fervour that was still alive in Lincolnshire after the campaigns of John Wesley. At revivalist meetings, preachers like Gypsy Smith and Peter Mackenzie went to work upon the unregenerate, after the sensuous tunes and the dramatic words of the Moody and Sankey hymn-book had so stupefied them with emotion that they were ready to believe anything. First came the lashing of the ungodly, then the vision of their appalling future, and finally, like the sun breaking through cloud, the sudden offer of redemption. All was made easy by the doctrine of salvation by grace. Instantaneous conversion was enough to lift a transgressor from the depths of wickedness to the pinnacles of beatitude. Indeed, the darker the sin, the brighter the light of salvation. The saints of evangelism were the greatest transgressors, and they were taken from meeting to meeting to tell the stories of their past. The best performances provoked storms of clapping and demands for encores. 'Say it again, Mrs Pivvy! Say it again!' was the cry my grandmother once heard after that lady had confessed to some particularly interesting pre-redemption experiences. Unfortunately, the effects of salvation were usually temporary and often a mixed blessing to the convert's friends and relatives, because if those living in a state of grace were well aware of their own previous shortcomings, they were even more conscious of the continuing deficiencies of others.

This great-grandfather of mine, John Fisher, had been apprenticed as a blacksmith to his father in Whatton, but as a younger son he went off to Sheffield to pick up a precarious living there outside his trade, after marrying the widow of a prosperous auctioneer in Gainsborough, called Dewick. Her maiden name was Mary Maitland, and it was through her that the supposed noble blood of Scotland had flowed into the Fisher veins before she died of consumption at the age of fifty, leaving two daughters by Mr Dewick— Polly and Bessie—and three children by John Fisher— Kate, Edward (my grandfather) and Pat. These five children did not burden Mary's widower for long. He proceeded to drive his adolescent Dewick stepdaughters, Polly and Bessie, from home as quickly as he could. His own daughter Kate left soon afterwards, determined to make her fortune— which she did. John Fisher was then faced only with the problem of how to foist off his remaining children, Edward and Pat, upon anyone who would have them. He solved it, when my grandfather was twelve, by taking the two children

on what became known in the family as 'the pilgrimage'.
Grandfather never forgot the itinerary. Chesterfield was the
first stage, where they stayed with James Maitland who, it
was reported, 'weren't ower glad t'see 'em', because he was
a highly respectable and pompous manufacturer of sanitary
fittings, with whom John had already deposited his step-
daughter Polly. He encouraged them to move on after one
night, and they continued on foot to Bulwell, near Nottingham, and there John Fisher's sister, who had married a
blacksmith, gave them shelter. The next trek was a short
one to Whatton, on the other side of Nottingham, where
they stayed at the blacksmith's house with John's elder
brother who had inherited the family business. Up to this
point John had been moving southwards, and had so far
tried one Maitland and two Fishers without finding anyone
to relieve him of either Edward or Pat. So now he decided
to strike north-eastwards to Hedingham where another
Maitland lived. The trio made that journey with two overnight stays, one at Caythorpe where John had friends, and
the other at Lincoln where he had reluctantly to pay for
lodgings. Eventually they arrived unannounced on Richard
Maitland's doorstep in Hedingham after a tramp of nearly
a hundred miles from Sheffield. Richard was then fifty. He
had one surviving daughter out of four, but no son. Therefore he was as glad to adopt his twelve-year-old nephew, and
to make him his apprentice, as the boy's father was to be rid
of him. The Hedingham master-blacksmith needed help in
his forge as well as on the several acres of land he owned
and farmed himself. Then John Fisher, having shed my
grandfather, went on with his daughter Pat to live in Gainsborough where he had met his wife; but as soon as Pat was
thirteen he put her out to service, which she hated. Within
a month she ran away to London and if her father ever
wondered what had happened to her there, he showed no
sign of being troubled by the uncertainty of her fate. For
her part, Pat felt under no obligation to acquaint so heedless
a parent of how she managed to survive alone in Victorian
London; but her brother Edward received from time to

time letters equivocal about her employment but at least assuring him that she was alive.

It was fifteen years before Pat was again seen by her relatives. My uncle Henry did not remember her reappearance because it was in 1884 when he was only two, but the details were well known to him because it was talked of for years afterwards in the village. His Aunt Pat suddenly appeared at the blacksmith's house in such a turn-out as Hedingham had seldom seen. She arrived in a carriage and pair, expensively dressed, bejewelled, and bearing the name of the Honourable Mrs James FitzPatrick. A very grand gentleman was her husband. He was tall and thin with elegant mustachios, and charmed everyone with his beautiful manners. Then, after a few brief but impressive calls amongst the Fishers and Maitlands, they returned to the metropolis where Pat assumed again the status of his one-eyed but delectable mistress. She had lost the sight of an eye as a child when she reached up to a shelf for the pepperpot. The lid came off and the pepper tipped into her eyes and on to her pinafore. In pain and fright Pat made her eyes worse by rubbing them with her pinafore, which was itself covered in pepper. One eye was so bad that the doctor neglected it while he preserved the sight of the other, but in spite of the loss of one eye—which she covered with a black eyeshade on elastic—Pat was very gay and pretty, with a pink and white rose-petal complexion. She grew up to be tall, vivacious and amusing. I first met her when she was an old spinster, gnarled and bent nearly double by rheumatism, but even then charm sparkled in her one eye, and to go and see her was a delight. What it was about Aunt Pat, who ought to have been ugly and repulsive, that made her so charming for a child to visit I don't know. It was not simply that she looked, with her black patch, like a disreputable old female pirate, nor even that her conversation was almost always covertly naughty and amusing. But whatever it was that Pat had, she had it in abundance.

On the subject of her situations in London she would chuckle and say, 'Yes, I was all right there for a time. But

I got disqualified.' Apart from these tantalizing references to her disqualifications, Aunt Pat remained for ever reticent about the detail of her life in the capital city, though she would tell the story of her running away. She took a train from Gainsborough with no luggage, no money, no knowledge of the world, and with no ticket. So all the way to London she dreaded the coming of the ticket collector and when nearing King's Cross she was dismayed by the sound of his approach. At the very last moment she had a sudden inspiration to say that she was in the care of the guard, and that satisfied him. Beyond that she would never tell, except that on arriving at the station she jumped on to the platform and 'ran and ran and ran'. She ran, at the age of thirteen, into the London of 1869, and not one word more would she ever say about it. When pressed, she would reply, 'That's my business.' After her first spectacular visit, Aunt Pat did not reappear in Hedingham until her sister Kate had made a fortune in America, and could afford to rescue Pat from London and Polly from her fate at the hands of the Chesterfield Maitlands. So I must now turn to this remarkable Kate Fisher, who not only changed the lives of Pat and Polly and kept my grandfather afloat from time to time with loans, but had a decisive effect upon my Uncle Henry's future.

Kate Fisher was fifteen at the time of her mother's death in 1865, and she left home not long afterwards to start work as a stewardess on ships of the Cunard Line plying between Liverpool and the United States. Her equipment for life was a total absence of beauty, a powerful drive, a good intelligence, no social graces whatsoever, and a marked generosity to all who were careful not to offend her. I have a photograph of Kate when she was fourteen. It is faded and brown with age but shows clearly enough a serious-minded young girl with wide-spaced dark eyes, and a large square forehead. Her hair is pale, parted down the middle, brushed closely over her ears and secured in the nape of her neck. Her lips are tight and, although her nose is large and broad, her face is dominated by a heavy chin. Every feature suggests determination and aggression, with the only hint of sexual appeal lying in the way her rather beautiful hair has a few loose strands escaping over her brow and lingering over her ears in its otherwise disciplined march to the back of her neck. After she had left home my grandfather and she corresponded regularly, and a few of her early letters survive.

They report objectively on her work and progress, calmly assessing within a year or two of starting work as a stewardess the possibility of earning higher wages in 'the States'. Perhaps these thoughts of improving her chances in the New World made her indifferent to retaining her employment with the Cunard Steamship Company because on one of her crossings she was bold enough to shoot the ship's captain with a revolver—not mortally, but at least she hit him in the leg and was discharged from the service in New York. My grandfather read a report of the incident in a newspaper and he later taxed Kate with a *crime passionnel*, because the report made clear, rather unnecessarily, that the girl herself was not being assaulted. For whatever reason Kate carried a revolver it could not have been to deter men from making love to her. However, the mystery of why Kate drew her gun was only deepened by her dismissal of my grandfather's accusation with a curt, 'There's no man on earth worth the price of a bullet.'

Finding herself turned off her ship in New York, Kate went out west and worked on a ranch in the Rockies, rounding up cattle on horseback. She must have learned to ride by experience, a method not recommended by Confucius. A pack of coyotes taught her to jump. They attacked a herd she was driving and the cows put their calves in the middle of a circle which they formed by standing with their horns outwards. That was an excellent defensive measure for the calves, but it left Kate out amongst the enemy, so she set her horse's head towards the menacing ring of horns, dug in her spurs, and held on as best she could. Fortunately her mount, having an equally strong incentive to join the calves, cleared the wall of cows as if bred for the Maryland Stakes and landed safely within the fortress. Thus Kate survived to leave the Rockies with a modest stock of capital from her savings as a cowboy, for she had, of course, spent nothing in the saloons. This capital she invested in a small celluloid factory, which soon went up in flames, leaving her penniless again. But my great-aunt had a spare string to her powerful bow. On one of her Atlantic crossings she had been the stewardess allocated to the state cabins of the Vanderbilts, and she ministered so efficiently to their ceaseless and complicated needs that even those exacting taskmasters never forgot her. So she had only to write to the Vanderbilts asking whether they had need of her services for them to offer her the post of stewardess on their private yacht in the Great Lakes. This was not the kind of job that Kate had any intention of holding for long. She was still determined to make her fortune as an entrepreneur, but the Vanderbilts would serve as a second spring-board after the initial disaster of the celluloid factory. On the Great Lakes, Kate quickly reingratiated herself with her millionaire employers, and was soon suggesting to them that their yacht lacked the facilities of a hairdresser and a masseuse, and that she herself could meet both needs after suitable training. Accordingly she was sent to Paris, at her employers' expense, to train at the best establishments. On her return she pummelled the Vanderbilt ladies and washed, cut and set their hair, all the time saving her wages for the day when she could leave their employment and set up in business again. She had to save for a long time, but eventually she was ready.

This time it was not celluloid, but beauty parlours. Her first salon was in Fifth Avenue in New York, and from there she exploded into Long Island, Avenue de la Paix in Paris, Bond Street in London, and the Via Condotti in Rome. She concocted and patented her own toilet preparations, and I have her book of recipes. The list includes : Old English Hair Tonic, Indian Herb Tonic, Sylphine in Jars, Cold Cream, Fairy Mist Liquid Powder, Oil Tonic for the Hair, Old English Shampoo Powder, Old English Shampoo Wash, Special Oil Tonic, Golden Shade, Skin Tonic, and Tonic de la Reine. The recipe for this last preparation will serve to demonstrate that Aunt Kate did not brew in small quantities. It reads :

Tonic de la Reine: Distilled water 12 gallons, witch hazel 12 gallons, alcohol 12 gallons. Perfume to suit with violet and jessamine. Colour green. A drying tonic for the moist hair and a good tonic for summer and seaside use. A dressing more than a grower.

It was the Old English Hair Tonic that was claimed to be the grower, and grow it did if my grandmother's experience is any guide. After an illness, her hair fell out at the back of her head till she was horrified to discover that she had a bald patch as large as her hand. When Aunt Kate was alerted to this disaster, she sent a supply of Old English Hair Tonic, which Mary nightly dabbed on to the itching patch and rubbed it well in. Within a month the affected area had sprouted a fine crop of chestnut brown hair, while the rest of grandmother's head was grey, making her wish that the disaster had been more widespread. In time, the new growth went grey and the final outcome was entirely satisfactory. However, lest I am importuned by the bald and credulous for the recipe, I will say that this preparation had a secret ingredient, the knowledge of which, if it ever existed, has gone to the grave with the inventor. Aunt Kate's manuscript recipe book makes no mention of secret ingredients, and their existence only came to light after her death when Henry, as her executor, was asked by Mr Roberts of Bond Street, who was running short of stock, to attend a mixing. When all the recorded ingredients had been poured into the vat, Mr Roberts discreetly withdrew saying that Henry could now be alone to add the last, which was obviously assumed to be something that could be secreted about the person. Henry hid his surprise, and after an interval recalled the agent to tell him that the job had been done. Thereafter for each new mixing he did the same, but whether on account of changing fashion or because the absence of something essential had taken the virtue out of Aunt Kate's preparations, sales dwindled after her death until in the nineteen thirties the royalties had become negligible.

On her ceaseless travels between the new and the old world, Kate descended regularly upon her relatives in Hedingham. She was now middle-aged, and short and fat, with bulgy feet in tight little boots. Her round pudding face was made up with pink liquid powder in a bottle. She had little dark snapping eyes, a gold tooth, and fluffy hair which never went grey because she dipped it in a mixture of strong cold tea and alcohol, the best hair-dye she had discovered. She always dressed in silk and, my mother said, 'exuded the loveliest scent of powder and perfume'. The pervading smell was of violets. On her arrival at the Glebe, old Thomas Millson and my mother were moved out of the best bedroom to share rooms with others, and the whole family was on its best behaviour till she left. My mother said that it was particularly nice to be well-behaved to one's important relatives, but I suspect that her recollections in this respect were more doctrinal than truthful. The children, however, loved their Aunt Kate for her generosity and knew that it would dry up if they offended her, so they did not—and gifts were showered upon them. She brought pearl and coral necklaces, little bags made of exotic brown beans, huge boxes of sweets and chocolates. Above all, she came loaded with supplies of her own preparations and trade publications. The stocks of toiletry at the Glebe were enormous, and my mother left home when a young woman with enough boxes of Old English Shampoo Powder to last well into my childhood. For years I had my hair washed with it, long after it had disappeared from the shops, and I remember the little oblong packets each with the name 'Kate Fisher' in old-fashioned script and her trademark—the head of a woman with lustrous long wavy hair streaming out in an unnatural fashion from each side of her head. The fine granules were brown, like curry-powder, and had to be mixed with hot water in a jug before the shampoo could be poured over the head. I hated it because the packets claimed truthfully that it curled the hair, and I longed for mine to grow straight. Although the preparations survived for many years, Kate's publications were all lost; but Henry remembered a small lavender-coloured pamphlet called *One Word Allow Me*, which gave a list of her patrons. They included the Queen of Greece, Lady Curzon, wife of the

86

Viceroy of India, the Duchess of Marlborough, Dame Nellie Melba and the Vanderbilts whose custom she had retained. Melba hired Aunt Kate to travel with her to Australia on a yacht to look after her hair and to keep her flesh within the bounds of her dresses, particularly her fabulous jewel dress for *Faust*. It was a hard job, but the voice that emerged from that excess of tissue must be one of the sweetest the world has ever heard, if Dame Nellie's surviving records, like the remote disembodied voice of a medium, are not as incredible as they sound.

The Duchess of Marlborough was the former Miss Consuelo Vanderbilt who, as a beautiful child of seventeen, was pressed by her parents to marry Charles Richard John, the ninth Duke, who was avid for her and for her money. Both passions are easy to understand, because I have a photograph of her head and shoulders which was autographed for Aunt Kate with 'Consuelo Vanderbilt 1895'. The pose is unusual, for she was photographed from behind, with her head turned towards the camera, as if the photographer had stolen up behind her and she had looked round to see who it was. Consuelo is wearing a white filmy dress, very low on the shoulders with a profusion of white flowers encircling the top. Round her long neck is a wide band of white silk tied at the back in a bow. The dark hair that Kate had dressed is swept up high to just below the crown of her head, where it is secured by a bow of ribbon set about with artificial flowers. Her mouth is full, her nose slightly uptilted, her eyes are large, dark and shrewd under very high arched eyebrows, as if raised in surprise at her parents' fondness for the English nobility. In developing the negative, the photographer obliquely suggested that the Duke would find Consuelo as he expected by printing an ornate roccoco frame round her head and shoulders, as if she were the Virgin Mary in a devotional painting. His Grace had every reason to adore that little heiress, but she detested him. Nevertheless, with those calculating eyes, Consuelo herself was not entirely insensible to the charms of a title, so she consented ; and Kate accompanied her to give aid to

87

her hair and comfort to her soul when she came over to England in 1895 for the wedding. According to my great-aunt, Consuelo swore to be divorced from the Duke as soon as she had borne him a few children, and *Burke's Peerage* records that she was as good as her word. She brought herself in 1897 to allow the Duke an heir, and in the following year another son as a reserve. Then Consuelo felt that she had done all that could reasonably be demanded of her, and departed. She was not divorced until 1921 when the Duke wished, surprisingly, to marry another American. His second union was given civil recognition in a registry office a few months afterwards, but the Duke had to wait another five years before the Sovereign Pontiff, as *Burke's Peerage* calls him, relieved him from the continuing sin of adultery by mendaciously and expensively declaring null and void the at least twice consummated marriage to Consuelo.

The Vanderbilt connection benefited the Fisher children as well as Aunt Kate. All the ladies of the millionaire household wore their clothes only once or twice before discarding them, so Kate bought them cheaply second-hand and despatched them in crates to her impecunious relatives. My Aunt Matilda spoke of the excitement when there was a message from Kirton station saying that a box from America had arrived. Grandfather got out the waggon and went to fetch it. Then it was opened on the living-room floor to disclose dresses with Worth labels, dozens of pairs of silk stockings, white brocade dressing-gowns, white lace gloves, shoes, coral beads, hats, furs, and everything expensive. Satins and silks predominated. Almost all the skirts were lined with stiff white taffeta that rustled whenever the wearer moved. In one box there were ostrich feathers in such profusion that even the children wearied of the gorgeous plumes and they were given to the maid. There were great heart-burnings when grandmother distributed the spoils, which arrived twice a year. Grandfather looked on, thinking of the smooth limbs that only recently had given shape to the gossamer stockings, and of the delicate arms that had filled the long gloves; his nostrils twitching under the assault of musk and civet-cat in the scents that still lingered in the luxurious garments. For herself grandmother kept little, realizing with her unfailing good sense that *haute couture* was not for a farmer's wife who made her own butter and went to chapel; although she was to be seen on occasions riding in the trap in a Vanderbilt blue cape with a storm collar lined with white fur. Mary was her mother's favourite and this, coupled with a certain arrogance and force of temper, enabled her to come off best and to go about the village in superb clothes that also fitted her. On the other hand, Henry had recollections of Matilda appearing in Hedingham Church, to his deep shame, in the most flamboyant and ill-fitting silks and satins entirely unbecoming to her age and surroundings, but of a quality that put anything that the Pitt-Melvilles could muster well into the shade. There was no question of my grandmother spending time on altering these clothes, or cutting them down to fit her daughters. It was one of her cardinal principles, like refusing to draw fowls, that she would neither sew nor knit. A little simple mending she would do, but in what leisure she had she hoisted her flag of independence, and read. The girls' clothes were made by Miss Way, an itinerant dressmaker, who came to stay at the farm for a week or so before the chapel anniversary, which marked the date for an annual new dress. Then she measured, cut out, sewed, fitted, and departed; but her clothes were rough and uncomfortable, making the Vanderbilt cast-offs a very welcome relief.

The Fisher children were grateful to their aunt for her generosity, but they could never be charmed by her. Although she had travelled all over the world, and had been a cowboy, a more uninteresting talker could not be found. My Uncle Henry claimed that she could have made being captured by Red Indians sound as exciting as taking tea with the Kirbys. She was always austere and business-like. Her conversation was often pungent, though never witty. Henry did not once see her laugh nor show any sign that she could smile, but she was kind and very much concerned for the welfare of her relatives. It matters little whether she was truly benevolent as my mother supposed, or loved power as my grandfather believed. For whatever reason, as soon as she had made enough money, Kate determined to find her half-sister Polly and her sister Pat, and to rescue them if necessary. Having seen her other half-sister Bessie on one of her visits to Athens, she knew that she was in no need of help. So Kate took the train to Chesterfield to discover that Polly, left by her father in the Maitlands' care, and been put into the workhouse. Her comment upon the head of that branch of the family was : 'James Maitland looks like a nobleman, and behaves like one.' Leaving Polly in the workhouse, but with assurances that her lot would soon be improved, Kate next set about finding her sister Pat in London, for she had resolved that they should be settled together in Hedingham. Tracing Pat was more difficult, but agents eventually found her living with a Mrs Ball in poor quarters in the East End. By now Pat was fifty and had added to the patch over one eye a broken nose acquired in a fight off the Whitechapel Road, and severe rheumatism contracted from working in a laundry. Even so she had no great wish to be rescued. She loved her disreputable friend Mrs Ball, and much preferred the London she knew to the Hedingham she had only visited once so splendidly and untruthfully in her heyday. However, Kate's will prevailed. She bought a comfortable little house by Hedingham beck and named it Wee Holme. She hired a resident maidservant, furnished the house, and installed Pat and Polly there with ample annuities. Polly, at least, lived blissfully in Wee Holme. She wore pale grey silk dresses with Brussels lace down the front. She sat in state in the sitting-room in a large wooden grandfather chair, with a maid in cap and apron to wait on her, and never did another stroke of work for the rest of her life. The simple-minded Polly was easily pleased, particularly after a long spell in the Chesterfield workhouse. She endorsed everything Kate said with 'Yus, sister,' except on very rare occasions when she turned obstinate and cantankerous beyond belief with the pig-headed intransigence of the rather stupid.

However, whereas Polly took to her new home with delight and gratitude, Pat was unhappy and restive. She despised Polly's easy contentment and resented Kate's charity. She pined for the colour and warmth of her old life with Mrs Ball, so Kate consulted my grandfather on what should be done. 'Let her go,' he advised, 'she'll soon come back.' And Pat went, returning to Hedingham within a few weeks and never again wanted to leave. Kate then bought her a large Mason and Hamlin harmonium, with a pianola attachment, and arranged for Miss Abbey, the chapel organist, to teach her to play. In spite of the rheumatism in her fingers, Pat mastered hymns and other simple tunes. She delighted in her new accomplishment and in the row of organ stops that brought in flutes, clarinets, hautboys and *vox humana* to enliven the tunes of the Anglican hymnal. For more demanding works, such as Sousa's marches, the overture to *Zampa*, and Weber's *Euryanthe*, she could slide back a panel in the top of the harmonium to reveal the pianola. All she had to do was wind the clockwork, fit one of her large stock of rolls, pump the foot pedals, and use her knees to press the flaps that could invoke gentle or sudden crescendos and diminuendos within a range extending from a fortissimo that shook the house to a pianissimo that was barely audible. Whatever frustrations Pat may have retained in a rural environment she could amply release when seated at so powerful and versatile an instrument. Kate's insight in choosing such a present to mark Pat's return to the family is an indication not only of an intelligence and generosity that were often displayed, but of a sensibility that she seldom allowed herself to reveal.

After settling Polly and Pat in Hedingham, Aunt Kate decided to buy a house there herself as a *pied à terre* in which she could later live in retirement. Although she had taken out American nationality it was only to further an expatriate career. England was still her natural home and she would have felt a greater sense of achievement to have made money in her native country than in the United States. Anyone born poor tends to respect commercial success at home because his parents so obviously missed it. For this reason Kate could not wholly admire even the Vanderbilts because they had emigrated to make their millions. She regarded Nabob money as second-class money in everything but purchasing power. 'Henry!' she once said, 'Although I couldn't make money in England, I can at least spend it here. I hope you, my boy, have enough brains to do both.' There was little need to express those sentiments to her nephew. He had been brought up to have no ambition to be rich abroad. His father would have accepted a gift of a thousand acres in Nebraska, but only to use the rents to buy English land, not to become an exiled farmer. Indeed, his ambitions were narrower than that. My grandfather's ideal acres would march with those of the Andersons and Kirbys, but further. My grandmother was the same. Between her love of one Edward Fisher and her marriage to the next she had for twelve years been a cook, and her pastry-making was so exceptional that an American guest at one of her places of employment had offered to set her up in business with a patisserie in New York, but she declined. Emigration was for the unfortunate Irish, and she would stay and take her chances at home. As for Henry, he had already set his sights on Lincoln. That was where he intended to make his fortune, in the county town where his multitude of cousins could not fail to take notice, even if a few of them had strayed beyond the borders of Lincoln-shire into Nottingham and Chesterfield. In one sense this Fisher ambition to succeed at home was petty; but in an-other it was arrogant because they truly believed, and with some justification in a period of agricultural depression, that it was easier to make money elsewhere. For this reason Aunt Kate was always modest about her achievement. While she used the power of her money, and enjoyed using it, she could never allow herself to feel superior to those who had struggled less successfully than she, but in the same environment that had defeated their parents. Furthermore, Kate shared the Fisher attachment to their roots that went down deep into the Lincolnshire ground. On her visits to

England she had pored over church registers, tracing so far as she could in those exasperating records—bedevilled by fires, plagues, negligent parsons and Nonconformist baptisms—the broken threads of her ancestry. She had particularly sought to prove the nobility of the Maitlands, but she only found that they had petered out in the Hedingham registers leaving no trace of where they had come from. This, however, did not deter my great-aunt, when she had progressed a little in the world, from executing a deed poll conferring upon herself the accolade of Kate Maitland Fisher, instead of the plain Kate Fisher of her baptism.

It was enough for the earliest recorded Maitland ancestor to have lived in Hedingham to establish it as the natural home of the family. So Polly and Pat were settled there willy-nilly and Kate started to look for a suitable house for herself in the same village. Eventually she bought the Grange from Uncle Charlie Rudkin who had lived there until his father died. Before Aunt Kate started to improve it, the Grange was a modest Lincolnshire red-brick farmhouse with a pan-tiled roof and the restful charm of its kind. After she had finished, only a small east wing survived, and only that because it was largely out of sight and served to provide a scullery and other humble domestic offices. The remainder of the house was rebuilt and enlarged into a hideous villa, with half-timbered gables, decorated brickwork, contorted chimney-stacks, rectangular bay windows, and an ornate porch. The most that can be said in extenuation is that Kate was at least in the van of contemporary taste, because her concept of the best in domestic architecture soon spread like a rash throughout the more prosperous parts of England. Scorning the services of an architect, Kate designed the new Grange herself and suffered the usual consequences. A substantial part of the house had been rebuilt before she realized that she had miscalculated the amount of space required for a staircase, so the new construction had to be pulled down again, or she could never have got up to bed. Other oversights also obliged her to alter the plans many times as the work proceeded ; but in the end the house was completed at great, largely unnecessary, and certainly ill-conceived expense. All the windows had been glazed with plate glass with bevelled edges, and after Kate went into residence she found that the sun threw all the colours of the rainbow over her expensive pictures and wallpapers, till she was driven to distraction by 'the damned prisms' and had cheap glass put in instead. The drawing-room opened through french windows into an orangery, like a miniature Crystal Palace, with a Gothic arched roof, in which the oranges never ripened in spite of a prodigious application of heat. Later it became the orchid house. Along the south front of the house ran an Italianate loggia with classical columns, in which Kate could sit on summer evenings and admire the orchard she had planted with the fruit trees, against repeated advice, too close together. The interior of the house was lavish with exotic woods and intricate plaster to provide a proper setting for the collection of paintings, marbles, china, glass, gilt and silver she had acquired on visits to Italy and Greece. Her more ornate furniture came from Paris. For the remainder, Maples in London preserved her from anything simple and beautiful. Liberty's provided her fabrics, while Harrods made the curtains for her windows and the canopies over her beds. So there was nothing in the house of less than the highest quality, nor in less than dubious taste. The ostentation of the Grange contrasted sharply with the simple comforts of Wee Holme, where Polly and Pat lived as Kate's pensioners, but it was not for them to draw comparisons. The view of the family was that Kate had made her own money and was entitled to spend it, though my grandfather could not help but calculate by how much the Grange had impoverished Kate's ultimate legatees amongst whom, being younger than she, he presumed to hope to number. On the other hand, the Grange greatly enhanced the standing of the Fishers in Hedingham because at the turn of the century it was the kind of house that almost anyone in the village, except the Squire, the Rector and Mr Palfreyman, would have built for himself if he could.

Of the five children and stepchildren dispersed by John

Fisher, four of them—my grandfather, Polly, Pat, and Kate
—were now settled, or preparing to settle, in Hedingham,
where their mother Mary Maitland had been born. The
fifth, Bessie, was unable to complete the family reunion
because she lived in Athens, married to a Greek. However,
her daughter, another Kate, came to live at the Glebe for
almost a year, and while she was there she pushed forward
the frontiers of Henry's experience of music and her own
experience of men. Cousin Katie was the first to take Henry
down more than a peg or two, so she deserves a little introduction. She was also a fairly interesting character in her
own right. Henry and she shared the grandmother, Mary
Maitland, who first married a Mr Dewick, by whom she
had Bessie and Polly. Then Mr Dewick died and his widow
married John Fisher, taking Bessie and Polly to live with
him. That was not much to Bessie's liking because her
father had been a gentleman, and her stepfather was not. It
was freely acknowledged within the family that Mary Maitland married well the first time and badly the second; they
assumed that she remarried for love, because John Fisher
had nothing else to offer. Little was remembered of Mary
Maitland except that she had a passion for chemistry. I have
to this day, as a memento of her, two of the jars with ground-
glass stoppers in which she kept the copper sulphate, ferric
oxide and other materials for her experiments. When she
died in 1865, her daughter Bessie was eighteen and did not
stay with her stepfather any longer than was necessary to
see her mother buried. That done, she sailed with a family to
Greece as their nursemaid, and in Athens soon improved
her position by becoming nursery governess to the royal
family of Greece. In that capacity she met a young English
naval officer, and they fell in love. Unfortunately duty soon
called him away, and he sailed from Greece having promised
to return and marry her. For a time they corresponded, then
suddenly his letters stopped and hers received no answer.
In the end, being wooed by a Greek hotel proprietor called
Petro Polynopoulos who vowed to marry her in spite of her
reluctance, she gave up hope of ever hearing again from her

lover and married Petro. Then, little more than a month after the wedding, the naval officer returned to make good his promise. A blockade had been the explanation of his enforced silence. 'In those days,' said my Aunt Matilda, 'there was no running away when once married. So that was that !'

It was some consolation for Bessie that Petro proved to be a kind, generous and devoted husband. He had fallen in love with the back of Bessie's neck where dark chestnut-brown wavy hair curled into the smooth white Maitland skin. That was only one of Bessie's charms. My mother said, and allowance must be made for her enthusiasms, that Aunt Bessie was the loveliest woman she had ever seen. She had beautiful eyes and teeth, a straight nose and a charming smile. Her voice was soft and bantering and, unlike her half-sister Kate, she was a wonderful story-teller. If anything detracted from her beauty it was the smallest hint of the Maitland cast in her left eye. What certainly detracted from her otherwise charming character was the meanness that she shared with her sister Polly. 'The Dewick sisters', said my Aunt Matilda, 'were as mean as tea in a tin.' In contrast the Fisher pair, Kate and Pat, 'would give their heads away'. However, Petro Polynopoulos worshipped Bessie, and they lived happily together although he knew that she pined for her lost sailor. Their daughter Katie was born in 1876, and before she was a few months old the Queen of Greece, who well remembered her mother's charm and efficiency, was insisting that Katie should have an education designed to fit her to become a principal governess to the royal children. So, partly at the expense of the Greek Exchequer and partly at Petro's, Katie had an international schooling in Paris, Berlin, Geneva and Florence, which added fluent French, German and Italian to her native Greek and to the English her mother had taught her. As if that were not enough for the royal children, Katie's natural talent for the piano was developed at an academy in Vienna run by Paderewski, where she was made to practise for six hours a day with coins on her wrists to prevent her from throwing her arms extravagantly about, as she would otherwise have done, and did again as soon as she could. Paris provided the finishing school, and there she was taken up by Aunt Kate on her business visits, until the young girl was careless enough to offend her. Aunt Kate was accustomed to allow her niece the freedom of her hotel account to entertain her titled friends from the school. On the last of these occasions Katie expressed to her companions, in English, the hope that 'the old thing wasn't about'. She might have hoped more devoutly than she knew, because the old thing was about and heard through an open door. Aunt Kate lived up to her reputation for never forgiving, and as my mother said, 'Not one more brass farthing ever again came Katie's way from that direction.'

Katie also did not scruple to offend the royal family of Greece. The consequence of all her fine education was that she declined to become a governess, even to royalty. Instead she determined, since her mother had failed, to marry an Englishman. Unfortunately there were not many in Athens, and the only one she could find was a Cook's courier, showing tourists round the Acropolis, called Fred Mordell who, being away from home, was able to give a better account of his circumstances and prospects than the truth warranted. There was nothing else that could have commended him, except his rarity, to a clever and highly educated girl, blessed with good looks and a fine figure. Kate was not quite so beautiful as her mother because Petro's genes had darkened her complexion, slightly widened her nose, and allowed a hint of the Levantine to cloud the innocence of her English eyes. Nevertheless she could have tempted into matrimony a far better specimen of mankind than Fred Mordell. My Aunt Matilda remembered him as 'attenuated', being tall and thin with a small pointed beard and a bald head. It was also recalled that the only present he ever gave Katie was 'a wilted bouquet'. Indeed, the family's reaction to poor Fred was extremely unfavourable. They even went so far as to associate his attenuation with Katie's post-marital behaviour at the Glebe. As for her parents, they were bitterly opposed to the match, but Katie was head-strong. Petro's sad comment was, 'Katie one little fool. She cost me two thousand pound.'

She was nineteen when she came to the Glebe on her honeymoon in 1895. Fred Mordell's job as a courier took him all over the world, but his base was in England, so he brought his wife there as Katie had intended. However, far from being able to provide her with a house in London, he could not even afford a proper honeymoon, so they went to stay with my grandfather in Hedingham, where Katie remained for nearly a year. The extent of my grandfather's hospitality is surprising because he was both short of money and mean. Also, there was not much room at the Glebe for visitors. The house had eight bedrooms, but they had to serve for husband and wife, old Thomas Millson, eight children, a resident maid, and two resident farm labourers —fourteen people. Whenever the Fishers had guests, Thomas and my mother were shifted out of the best bed-room and others had to make room for them. Yet the Glebe was open house to relatives down to second and third cousins. Maitlands from Chesterfield and Hornsea stayed when they wished and for as long as they felt inclined. So did Fishers from Whatton, Nottingham and Bulwell. Mill-sons came from Ludford, Gainsborough, Market Rasen, and as far afield as Hartlepool in Durham and Grays in Essex. The reason for this apparently prodigious hospitality was that it was reciprocal and provided the only means of ever having a holiday. No one in the family could afford to stay at an hotel, so on the rare occasions when a Fisher left the Glebe for a destination from which he could not return by nightfall, it was to stay with an uncle or a cousin. Relatives' houses were like monasteries in the Middle Ages where one could always find shelter, and Katie Mordell did no more than take rather extended advantage of the system.

Even on his honeymoon, Fred was drinking a bottle of whisky a night which, needless to say, he provided; and Katie was already showing signs of a dissatisfaction that my grandfather did not fail to observe. After an uneasy fortnight, Fred resumed his travels and went on a tour of Norway, unwisely leaving his wife behind at the Glebe with time on her hands. She filled it in a variety of ways. One of her activities was to iron her fine and expensive clothes interminably and with extraordinary delicacy. Another was to dress a doll. Every stitch in this doll's clothing was hand-sewn. Every piece of clothing could be taken off, for it was fitted with little pearl buttons and dainty loops. The dress was of pink nun's veiling with pale green baby-ribbons, and when Katie eventually left the Glebe she gave the doll to my Aunt Matilda. Grandmother promptly put it away into the display cabinet in the sitting-room because she had never had a doll as a child, and she couldn't bear the thought of anything so beautiful being spoiled. One day Matilda stole it from the cabinet, and held it defiantly behind her back as her mother approached, threatening to punish her; but old Thomas intervened with, 'Nay, Bessie! She's but a bairn!' Nevertheless, the doll was restored to its sanctuary, and Matilda never touched it again. The deprivation of that un-believable present earned for her mother the one really heartfelt grudge that Matilda ever bore against her.

Otherwise, Katie's leisure was mainly filled with music. The piano-tuner from Kirton was summoned to give the old Collard and Collard, with its fretted front, a particularly good tuning, and to replace the exhausted strings in the bass. Then by day the unaccustomed action had to galvanize itself to meet the demands of Beethoven, Schubert, Schu-mann, Chopin, Liszt, Brahms and Wagner. Katie was nothing if not a romantic. In the gloaming, however, when the daylight was fading outside and a fire was flickering in the living-room with flames leaping from the burning coals, Katie set herself like a good guest to entertain her hostess. The hanging lamp was not lit earlier than three hours before bedtime because it did not hold enough paraffin, and it was dangerous to top up the bowl while the wick was alight. This left a period of gloaming when grandmother would sit in the growing darkness at the end of the couch next to the piano, and Katie played from memory or by ear the popular tunes her hostess loved, including the 'Blue Danube', 'Robin's Return', 'In the Shade of the Sheltering Palm', 'After the Ball', Gavotte from *Mignon*, 'Melodie d'Amour'. Katie would sing to her, too, in a light contralto, because it happened that her voice was exactly as my grandmother would have wished. It was clear, unaffected and innocent of technical tricks, for grandmother had the greatest contempt for a trained singer. Any local girl with a sweet voice who took singing lessons was ruined so far as she was concerned. Fortunately Katie's voice was as untutored as a blackbird's, since no one in Vienna had thought it worth improving. Thus it was well suited to the sorrowful and nostalgic songs expected of her—'Ben Bolt', 'The Miller's Daughter', 'Listen to the Mocking Bird', 'In the Gloaming', 'Oh my Darling !' There were dozens of soul-aching memories for one who had been disappointed in love, particularly a dreadful dirge ending :

'Tis better to have loved and lost
Than not have loved at all.
Love ! I will love for ever !

Katie was not disposed to be melancholy for her departed husband, and tried to prise my grandmother out of her taste for the mournful, but it was no use. All the songs had to be sad and sentimental, and grandmother sat enjoying her induced misery as darkness deepened and the moon rose pale in the east, lifted over the trees, and flooded the lawns with silver.

After supper, with the whole family at home, Katie went to the piano again to rattle off anything that anyone wanted. My mother would be upstairs in bed, enjoying the lively tunes until Katie was asked to open the Moody and Sankey hymn book. Then her misery began. There was a family male voice quartet of Henry, John, James and grandfather, with John singing the alto line falsetto. The revivalist hymns in four parts oozed up from below her to reduce my mother to a sobbing squirming melancholy—'Oh ! Where is my Boy Tonight?'; 'Throw out the Lifeline!'; 'Someone is Smiling'; 'When the Dewy Light is Failing'. These maudlin tunes could leave Fanny in a quaking agony till, by the time Katie left the Glebe, the sound of any music at all welling up from downstairs after my mother had gone to bed could make her miserable.

Although it was rarely that Henry was free from school or work on the farm to play his fiddle with Cousin Katie, she had gone into Lincoln to arm herself with a set of Beethoven's violin sonatas, all three of Brahms's, and a few of Schumann's. This was new territory for Henry because the Rector's range of appreciation ended with the eighteenth century. Early Beethoven he could tolerate, but the Grosse Fugue and the Ninth Symphony he found frenetic. For him the tension of a work of art was lost when the emotional pressure was allowed to escape from the restraint of a strict form. 'Chopin', he used to say, parodying at the piano a few bars of a nocturne, 'reminds me of nothing so much as spilled treacle spreading where it will all over the floor.' Tchaikovsky he called 'the Russian invertebrate'. As for Brahms, Wolf and Bruckner, he heard with delight that when they were living in Vienna at the same time, each of them detested the other two. 'I heartily agree,' he said, 'with all three!' Therefore Henry's ear was not attuned to the romantics; but Katie rushed him nevertheless through a good deal of the nineteenth-century sonata repertoire, which was too difficult for him, calling out when he faltered, 'Keep going! Aim for the end of the run! Don't lose the rhythm! Good! Good!' But Henry did not enjoy it. Katie was too much for him in a musical way, as she was for her husband in another. He had, at the age of twelve, neither the technique nor the experience to sight-read the violin parts at the speeds that Katie found easy and natural on the piano. Since he had no time to practise the music in advance, he was always at a disadvantage. So his experience of sonatas with his Greek cousin was a cold wind from Europe that nipped the buds of self-esteem that had sprouted too early and too vigorously in the shelter of a

Lincolnshire village, in which few could play at all and none well enough to make young Henry Fisher feel uneasy in comparison. He expected eventually to play as well as the Rector, and Katie was his first encounter with hopeless competition. If she had been a concert pianist, it would have been easy to bear, but Katie was not in the first rank. Even so, she was too good for him, and he remembered her with more respect than affection. 'By God,' he told me, 'I felt like a milk float harnessed to a racehorse!'

His eldest brother John, on the other hand, was not in the least intimidated by Katie, because what she required of him he could easily supply. 'My brother John was the only handsome one in the family,' said my mother with characteristic modesty. I never saw Uncle John to remember him, because he died in his fortieth year before I had attained my first, but a huge oak-framed photograph of my grandmother's favourite son hung over the fireplace in her living-room. It confirmed reports of the almost too perfect good looks of this Apollo of the north-west Lincolnshire escarpment. They were also confirmed by his two children, a very handsome boy and a girl so beautiful that she became a film actress, until the silent films were replaced by talkies. Then my lovely cousin Dinah, being too proud to surrender her Lincolnshire accent to a teacher of elocution, was obliged to retire into matrimony and the arms of a rich man who was sufficiently content with her other attributes to allow her to pronounce 'castle' as she pleased. The father of these two beautiful children was only sixteen when Katie Mordell appeared at the Glebe, but his clear blue eyes, entirely regular features, and curly brown hair had already been taking their toll amongst the girls of Hedingham. That Katie was three years older than he did not prevent her from falling another victim to his attractions, and the speed of her capitulation was naturally attributed to her brief and disappointing experience of matrimony with poor Fred. Within a week of his disappearance on tour, Katie and John were slipping away together from the Glebe whenever the weather was fine and opportunity served, returning from fields and barns with the unmistakable air of content of those who have recently and happily made love. John was betrayed by the spring in his step, the hint of a smile on his lips and an ill-disguised buoyancy of spirit. Katie told all by the way she sank into a chair, stretched out a limb, or yawned lazily at supper. As my Aunt Matilda said, 'They were at it before Fred's ship was over the horizon !' Yet my mother was most reluctant to concede that any girl of careful upbringing and good education could simply be subject to the demands of the flesh. She maintained, in supposed mitigation of Katie's intemperate adultery, that she fell 'deeply in love' with her handsome cousin. Be that as it may, even my mother could not believe that Katie also fell in love with my grandfather. That had to be accepted as behaviour on a very different level of turpitude.

I do not know why Katie, and many others, were unable to resist my grandfather. He was a good-looking man, tall and impressive ; but neither a fascinating talker, nor in-gratiating and charming. Nevertheless he did not rape the adolescent servant-girls at the Glebe, nor anyone else. Either they fell into his arms, or he let them be, but often they fell into his arms. I can only think that he had a talent for seduction as innate as a gift for mathematics. Indeed, he never ceased to be surprised by his success with women and loved to talk about it, making an unwilling confidante of his daughter Matilda, partly because he enjoyed shocking her, and partly because he sensed that she would be too scandalized to repeat the stories of his conquests to her mother. 'He insisted on telling me everything,' said Matilda, 'the dirty old beast !' Later, grandfather and my father used to exchange accounts of their experiences, and analysed them as earnestly as a couple of social scientists. Grand-father formed very clear ideas on how women should be treated in amorous encounters, having rationalized his own inclinations, as we all do. He believed, like Montaigne, that man's highest pleasure lies in pleasing his partner. To that extent he was a considerate and unselfish lover ; but he was also convinced that women do not derive the highest erotic excitement in a loving relationship. Too many wives with devoted husbands had achieved at his casual hands the sexual fulfilment they had missed in affectionate matrimony for him to accept what he called the 'clap-trap' of the moralists. What really stimulated women was, in his opinion, a mating prompted simply by mutual desire, with no background of sentimental dalliance, no pretence of being in love, and no declarations of undying attachment. Of course, women had been taught by parents, parsons and other deceivers to believe that an emotionally cool but sexually white-hot relationship was not what they wanted. But in fact it was—as they discovered, with his co-operation, when they had experienced it. Therefore as soon as he had read the first signs—often disguised, often reluctantly conceded, sometimes apparently reversed—that a woman was interested in him as a man, he would if he found her desirable allow faint signals of his interest to reach her. This, the only preliminary stage, was on no account allowed to degenerate into anything so explicit as a flirtation. Then after an interval to assess the chances, his pride forbidding him to risk carelessly the probability of a rebuff, he decided whether to make an approach. If so, it was sudden, surprising and determined.

That was the pattern of his taking Katie Mordell. Her ineffectual husband and the boy John had awakened her to the possibilities of erotic pleasure, and grandfather began to intercept glances that he correctly identified as curiosity. She was wondering, as any woman recently loved by half a man and a boy was bound to wonder, what it would be like to be had by a man. So without much hesitation, grandfather decided that she should have the opportunity of discovering. One morning when he knew that grandmother was out in the village, he came in from the fields to the living-room, where Katie was playing Opus 28. He stood silently by the piano listening and watching as the tension between them mounted to a point where Katie's fingers began to fumble the E major arpeggios in the fourth movement. Then he lifted her arms from the keyboard, raised her to her feet, and kissed her. She clung to him as her heart raced and her breathing quickened until, knowing that she was his, he took her by the hand and led her up the staircase to her bedroom. There, after carefully arousing her passion, he assuaged it not once, nor twice, but three times, in a long leisured confident rhythm that was new in her limited experience. Thenceforth, though Katie did not abandon her cousin John, she lived longing for the moment when her host would again interrupt her playing and lead her to bed. She never knew when it would next be, for grandfather made no assignations. Always he took her by surprise and at fairly long and irregular intervals, because the farm had the first claim on his time, with others to share the few hours he could devote to pleasure. Although grandfather's attentions were spasmodic, John's were more regular and even Katie's husband visited the Glebe occasionally when he returned to England between his tours. It was as well that he did because after his wife had been in Hedingham for nearly a year she found herself pregnant and returned home to Greece. The boy was born there, and as his features began to assume one shape rather than another, Katie scanned them anxiously to read the indications of his inheritance, finding to her great relief that, if he had the look of anyone, it was of his Greek grandfather. So which of the three had made her pregnant Katie never knew. Fred assumed that the claim was his, but his travels never again took him to Greece, and he had neither the money to make a special journey to go see his offspring, nor the inclination to see his wife. Katie and he thenceforth lived apart, and though she returned to settle in England after her parents died, that was many years later, and not with Fred.

Katie Mordell had good reason to scrutinize her child's features to read the genetic story, but many women do it out of idle curiosity, and some men out of apprehension. With my grandmother it was a passion, because she had dearly loved the mother she had lost when she was six and the brother Jim who had died in his youth. Every son of hers, and later every male grandchild, to whom a Millson strain could even remotely be attributed was 'the image of my brother Jim'. Every female child, if only in the eye-lashes, took after her lost mother. Yet Henry defeated her. She could readily concede that he owed nothing to the Fishers and Maitlands on her husband's side, but even she could not claim that he was a Millson. There was no resemblance whatsoever in any of his features to the linea-ments of her brother Jim. It was not that Henry's coun-tenance was misshapen or ill-favoured. It was an ordinary face, and that was the trouble. All my grandmother's other children derived at least something from their ancestry, even if it was unfortunate like the Millson lower lip or the Maitland cast; but not her third son. 'My Henry,' she said with disgust, 'has the sort of face you might have bought, like a turnip, in Brigg Market.'

It was almost a fair description. Apart from a pair of bright blue eyes and a set of very white teeth, a little too widely spaced, there was nothing in his face to notice or remember. Even his hair was pale and thin and straight. When Katie left the Glebe, Henry was of ordinary height for his age of thirteen and of a nondescript build. In appearance he was wholly undistinguished, yet he was the most attractive boy of the family. Whilst John had the good looks, Henry had the charm. He was vibrant with energy, always in a hurry, bursting into a room to explode into a new story of some ridiculous incident in the village. He could mimic and mime till the family rolled over with laughter. Even now at the entrance to his teens he could lend interest and fascination to the most trivial anecdote. If there was a boring job to be done, like watering the garden, grandmother had only to put Henry on the watering can for the younger children to volunteer to carry the buckets from the pump. Everyone at the Glebe loved him and, strangely, none seemed jealous. Perhaps it was because grandfather thrashed and bullied him like the rest, and hid his conviction that Henry was the son who would ultimately make Fisher a name to conjure with amongst farmers in north-west Lincolnshire. One who did not hide that conviction was his uncle Charlie Rudkin, who had already asked to adopt him. He had been refused, of course, out of hand; but Charlie had a reputation for getting what he wanted. Henry himself had been won over. His schooldays had only strengthened his conviction that life had more to offer him than the general run of mankind, that he needed an education commensurate with his ability, and that only his uncle Charlie could provide it. So the battle lines were drawn up ready for Aunt Kate's decisive intervention, and the time has come for me to give shape and form to the man who was ultimately the victor and who made Henry the most eccentrically educated lawyer in Lincolnshire.

Charles Utting Rudkin was the son of John Rudkin, the Hedingham cordwainer, or bootmaker as he would now be called. John was notorious in my family for his querulous and inhospitable nature. When he was out it was the custom in winter for the idle villagers to gather in his workshop to chat with his journeymen while warming themselves before his fire. He came in once to find the shop too full and the fire blazing too merrily for his liking. He said that he could feel the heat of the fire in the cobbler's shop as he was coming down the Jossaway, on the other side of the village. Muttering 'constantly in jeopardy', he began to move everything he could lay hands upon away from the fire to the back of the building, as if there were imminent danger of a conflagration. When that demonstration failed to dislodge his unwelcome guests he went outside and climbed on to the roof to put a tile over the chimney pot, thus filling the shop with smoke until he had driven his callers out choking into the yard. The expression 'constantly in jeopardy' fell always from his lips whenever he encountered the obstructions and annoyances that life so carelessly leaves in our way, and a major source of jeopardy was his wife, Hannah Utting, who claimed to trace her family back to a Norman knight called Sir Dugard Utting. She was a tall, plain, gaunt, silent and expressionless woman, with a will as hard as rock. She sat bolt upright in her chair and looked, according to my Aunt Matilda, 'like an American backwoodswoman'. A story illustrates the quality of the matrimonial relationship that bred Charlie Rudkin. A villager once called at the cobbler's house to pay a bill and Mrs Rudkin took the money and gave him a receipt. The customer was a good one so she poured him a glass of whisky, and he was sitting in the parlour drinking it when her husband came home from buying some hides. 'So !' he cried on entering. 'You're giving your fancy man my whisky, are you? Well ! If my whisky's to be in jeopardy every time I leave my house, we know what to do about that !' He took the bottle and slowly drained in into the empty hearth. His wife was unperturbed. She went to the cupboard and, under the astonished gaze of the customer, crashed every bottle of spirits they had into the grate as well.

When Charlie was young he was as bad-tempered and aggressive as his parents. Like his supposed maternal ancestor, he loved fighting, and this future justice of the peace, county councillor, county chess player, grammar school governor and reader of the German philosophers in their original tongue was turned out of Hedingham School as unruly and unteachable. Thereafter he walked three miles each way daily to school in Redbourne where Mr Brierley found he could teach him nothing, until one morning, despairing, he gave Charlie paper and pencil and told him to go away and make a sketch of the village church. Charlie drew the church as best he could, and then sat on a tombstone and reflected. He took himself back in time to when the site was a field. When there were no yew trees, no graves, no gravel paths, no church. Before the foundations were laid someone had planned the building. Centuries ago, an individual in medieval clothes had calculated the depth of the footings and the thickness of the walls required to sustain the weight of the tower. Someone had worked out the size and shape of the stones in the chancel arch. Another had been well-informed about the strength of roof timbers made of oak. Slowly it dawned upon Charlie that the man, long dead, who had designed the nave was, in his small way, one of those of whom his schoolmaster often spoke. 'Most men,' Mr Brierley used to say, 'crawl through life on their bellies, filling them if they can. But a few, the great ones, have minds and imaginations. They fly up into the sky and dwell with the gods. We shall never do that, you and I. But read, you poor fools, read! At least know what it is like to be out of the mud. What it's like to be a Shakespeare, an Alexander or a Michelangelo.' Although the schoolmaster's examples of sky-dwellers varied from time to time—except that Alexander was always included— Charlie could not recall that the architect of Redbourne church had ever once been mentioned. From this he concluded that the others must be worth knowing. Thus Mr

Brierley set Charlie Rudkin on the road to scholarship. Ecclesiastical architecture became his first and abiding passion, as if in gratitude for the lesson it had taught him, but year after year he spread his net ever wider and gradually stocked his capacious mind with much of the usual lumber of Western civilization.

When Charlie left school at the age of thirteen, it was to sit at a bench in his father's cobbler's shop to learn the trade. In what leisure he had he read all the books he could borrow from his relatives, who were many, and their friends. He read out in the fields on summer evenings, or in bed in winter by the light of a candle. His real opportunities to study came only when his cantankerous old father died and Charlie inherited the house and business. This was in 1893 and Charlie was by then thirty-two. I have a studio photograph of him at that age, or perhaps a few years younger. In a high-breasted dark suit with a white cravat, he leans negligently upon a thin black walking-stick. He wears button boots, a curly-brimmed bowler hat, and a broad gold Albert with medallions. There is self-assertion in his pose, and more than a hint of self-satisfaction in the faintly mocking smile. Yet Charlie would have been wiser to restrict his portrait to the head and shoulders or to have sat hatless and cross-legged in one of the ornate armchairs that were the stock-in-trade of Victorian photographers. Then it would have been less obvious that his legs were too short for his body and that his head was too large for everything else. We should have been unaware that Charles Utting Rudkin had the proportions of a very young tadpole. My grandfather put it more brutally : 'If Charlie's legs had been any shorter, his behind would have brushed the ground.' Perhaps on that account Uncle Charlie had been unsuccessful with the village girls. Even his wife, Emily, did not love him. She was the daughter of Richard Maitland, the Hedingham blacksmith who had adopted my grandfather, so in their teens they had grown up together in the same house. This had led her to contract a painful and unrequited affection for her cousin who, unlike Charlie, was not only tall and elegant but secreted a cold concentrated unloving sexuality that made many women desperate for him.

However, Charlie seemed not at all to resent his bride's infatuation for his closest friend; and it was some consolation that Emily, as her father's only surviving child, soon inherited all his money amounting to several hundred pounds and provided Charlie with some very useful capital. In other ways, too, Emily did her best to be as good a wife as she was able in the circumstances. Fortunately there was no risk that my grandfather might, now that she could not mistake a sexual for a matrimonial proposition, start to take advantage of her weakness for him. Charlie's security in this respect was not my grandfather's sense of propriety, but Emily's plainness. She had to a marked degree the Maitland family cast that made an eye wander outwards from alignment with the other. Though much less disfiguring than a squint, it would have detracted from the beauty of a pretty woman, and Cousin Emily had too little store of that commodity for any deduction at all to leave her with enough to tempt my grandfather. Since Emily's left eye strayed inconsequentially everywhere, no one could guess what was in her mind, nor whether she was being sober or frivolous. Also she had on the very top of her head a heavy pile of fair fluffy hair that was always slipping sideways in a ludicrous fashion. These things combined to give her an involuntarily comic appearance which tended to obscure both her deliberate wit, with which she was well armed, and the fact that she was almost as well-read as her husband. Nothing, however, could obscure her meanness, and she worked her maids to death for what was, even in those days, a mere pittance. 'Bessie,' she once complained to my grandmother when about to hire a servant girl, 'she wants four pounds a year!' Emily was also as narrow-minded as she was close-fisted and exceedingly intolerant of sexual misbehaviour. No unmarried mother could look to her even for sympathy and the transgressions of her husband, and later of her daughter Louisa, were extremely ill-received. Consequently, my grandfather ought to have been anathema to her, but perversely she lived with the heartache of always loving him and he lived with the satisfaction of continually reminding his wife and family of the fact.

Uncle Charlie and Auntie Rudkin went to live in the cobbler's house that he had inherited from his father. It was at one end of a terrace of red-brick cottages, with two rooms downstairs and three rooms upstairs. The scullery with a sink and pump was in an adjoining outbuilding, and there all the water for the house was drawn and the dishes were washed. Otherwise, the main business of the house was conducted in the living-room where a coal fire in a well-polished iron grate warmed the room and heated a side oven. Indeed, the living-room was also Charlie's bathroom, and right up to the time when I went as a boy to stay with him he insisted on hanging his shaving mirror on the back of the door into the yard, in spite of decades of experience of having his life put in danger every time anyone opened the door to come in. He shaved with a cut-throat and one unlucky jolt might have been mortal, so his household were on tenterhooks to shout and warn anyone they heard approaching; and by these timely cries of alarm they managed to preserve his obstinate life. All meals were eaten in the living-room where they were cooked, but they were eaten with formality. Charlie's atheism did not deter him from saying grace nor, incidentally, from insisting that his wife should attend chapel. Everything in his house had to be scrupulously clean, particularly the cutlery, and he would throw spoons across the room if they were not polished enough to suit him. He was irritable and demanding generally in the house and retained in his domestic environment the quick temper he had shown as a boy, though as an adult he never quarrelled outside his immediate household. His wife bore his tantrums with cool detachment and serene unconcern. Even when he was particularly tiresome, she would do no more than sit with her left eye askew, her hair lop-sided, and say 'Charlie! Charlie!' very softly, as if she were chiding a child.

The second downstairs room, which would otherwise

have been the front parlour, became Uncle Charlie's study, and it was soon completely lined with books. Here he read omnivorously, sometimes far into the night, though when it was cold he would move to the living-room after the others had gone to bed and sit with his feet thrust into the side oven. Before long Charlie could read French and German fluently, though he had never heard them spoken and his pronunciation was execrable. Classical history provided names for his two cats, Cadmus and Harmonia, and the vestiges of a religious upbringing suggested Cherubim and Seraphim for their twin kittens which continually did cry. Yet in spite of all the hours he spent in study, Uncle Charlie found time to run the cobbler's shop very profitably with the help of a foreman-journeyman known as 'Cobbler Jack', whose feet were terribly deformed. His toes, according to my Uncle Robert, 'were where his heels ought to be'. It needed all Jack's skill to make a pair of boots in which he could hobble painfully to and fro across the cobbled yard between the house, where his master was exercising his mind, and the shop where Jack saw that his instructions were carried out by the other two journeymen.

The pursuit of learning led to the front door of the house falling into disuse because it would have opened into the sanctuary of Charlie's study. So the little garden between the front door and the village street was abandoned and became a neglected riot of Michaelmas daisies, lupins, peonies, Canterbury bells, delphiniums, larkspur, gladioli, goldenrod, honesty, foxgloves and shrub roses. They fought for survival against the untended weeds, and flowered as best they could in the shade of overgrown lilac, laburnum and philadelphus. The neglect of this small but conspicuous front garden was in sharp contrast to the rigorous and intensive cultivation of three acres of land behind a large barn which, with the house and the bootmakers' shop, closed three sides of the cobbled yard. The fourth side was open to the village street. The back garden was tended by a small team of gardeners under the supervision of a man called Sidney. Like Cobbler Jack he seemed to be without a surname, and like Jack he was lame, but not nearly so disabled. That was just as well because he suffered the additional misfortune of a harelip. Uncle Charlie was thought to employ the misshapen out of kindness of heart, and perhaps he did—certainly the two foremen were devoted to him for his benevolence. But my grandfather was much given to looking round ethical corners. 'Take Jack, for example,' he used to say, 'the only advertisement Charlie has ever needed for his cobbler's business! If Jack can make boots he can even limp in, everyone knows he can fit an ordinary pair of feet to perfection. And Sidney! Not only lame but harelipped into the bargain! Yet observe carefully that there's nothing wrong with any of Charlie's other men. The only two who limp and lisp are the overseers. Why?' At this point grandfather raised a hand for a moment's silence as a prelude to the approaching revelation. 'Because those two unfortunates can be relied upon to take a real pleasure in making the others work. Didn't the ancient Egyptians put eunuchs in charge of their labour gangs on the pyramids? Trust C. U. Rudkin to understand human nature!'

If it was Sidney who made the gardeners work, it was Uncle Charlie who gave the orders, and he loved his plants to be in long straight rows. Vineyards and hop fields would have been his delight. He rejoiced in lines of sweet peas stretching towards the horizon on a regular structure of evenly spaced bamboos interlaced neatly with twine. He would have anything in rows, even daffodils and geraniums, and he had no regard for any supposed distinction between flowers and vegetables. They were never mixed in the same row, but we were as likely to find Uncle Charlie's wallflowers next to his shallots as next to his antirrhinums. This sort of gardening was, however, only in conformity with village tradition. It was merely the scale of Charlie's drillsergeant horticulture, and the excellence of it, that made it so monstrous. People came from miles around to admire it, and he was regarded as one of the best gardeners in that part of Lincolnshire. The products of the three acres, and of the huge greenhouses, were despatched most profitably by train from Kirton Lindsey to the London markets, but the garden was primarily intended to give pleasure. On a warm summer evening Charlie's relatives and friends would be walked along straight paths between squads of beehives, not only to pick lustrous black grapes from the vines in the hot-houses but to revel in the total beauty of his creation.

Not content with bootmaking and market gardening, Uncle Charlie developed a third line of business. He perceived that the disadvantage of inedibility in an egg was severe—that a less than good egg could be disastrous for an hotel proprietor, who would pay a premium to reduce the risk. So instead of producing eggs, Uncle Charlie left that to others and went into the business of collecting them daily, testing them, and marketing them with a guarantee of freshness. Early every morning one of his men drove a cart round the neighbouring farms collecting newly laid eggs. They were brought home, where Auntie Rudkin and the maid washed them scrupulously and held up each egg to the light of a candle to check that it was unfertilized. Then, gleaming, sterile and beautifully packed, the eggs were put on the afternoon train from Kirton Lindsey and appeared next morning on the breakfast tables of the best London hotels.

In these various ways, Uncle Charlie made a modest fortune while leaving himself free to spend time in his study. As he made money, he saved it and invested his capital in local property—cottages and smallholdings—which he let. In his middle age he was reputed in my family 'to own half Hedingham', and his daughter Louisa used to take Henry on walks round the village to point out the extent of her father's possessions and her own expectations. She was Uncle Charlie's second child. The first, Caroline, died of consumption when she was two and he composed an epitaph for her tombstone in Hedingham churchyard which suggests that he had not at that time entirely abandoned the possibility of survival :

She is not dead, the child of our affection,
But gone into that school wherein she needs
No more our poor protection.

On Caroline's departure, Auntie Rudkin nearly died of grief and only recovered sufficiently to live thereafter in a state of chronic ill health, though she did it for a very long time. Then Louisa's birth laid her still more prostrate and Doctor Rainbird pronounced that she must never, for fear of her life, have another child. This meant that her husband must thenceforth abstain entirely from sexual intercourse— at any rate with Emily. Since her low condition was thought to be due to consumption, she was further advised to live and sleep as far as possible in the open air. So Charlie provided her with a summerhouse that could be turned around like a weathercock to keep her out of the teeth of the wind, and there she spent most of her days and all her summer nights. The inevitable consequence of Emily's enforced chastity and her banishment to the garden for most of the year was that Charlie consoled himself with Sarah Bell, the resident maid of all work. This *ménage à trois* worked reasonably well except that Sarah tended, from the security of her master's bed, to give herself airs; and whenever Auntie Rudkin was resolved to dismiss her for pertness she found that Uncle Charlie was adamant that his mistress should remain conveniently at hand.

The decision after Louisa's birth that Auntie Rudkin should have no more children meant that Uncle Charlie was deprived of the possibility of a male heir, so he had turned a would-be dynastic eye in the direction of his nephew Henry. The other Fisher boys—John, James, Robert and George—were well enough, but none of them ever came to borrow his books, and none of them worried about why he was unable to divide twenty-two by seven to anything but an infinite number of non-recurring decimals. The phases of the moon they accepted without question, and they were as uninterested in the extraordinary habits of his beloved bees as they were in the compromises of the

Gregorian calendar. It was Henry who asked the sharp questions; Henry whose eyes were wide open upon the world with astonishment; and Henry who was already coming to the sad conclusion that it would be impossible ever truly to understand anything. Charlie would have adopted him not long after Louisa's birth, but he only proposed the idea in the almost certain knowledge that his father and mother would not agree. Nevertheless, what little leisure Henry had from school and working in his father's fields was largely spent at the cobbler's house. So when he left school at the age of thirteen his uncle proposed that he should go live with him, work for a few hours a day in the garden and spend the rest of his time amongst the books in his study. Then when he was seventeen he could go to Lincoln to seek his fortune. Henry was all for the proposition. Even my grandmother agreed; but grandfather would not hear of it. He needed Henry on the farm. Any of the others Charlie could have, 'but not the best of the litter'. Since that was the only one his cousin wanted, it was deadlock; and Charlie bided his time till Aunt Kate next came home. Then he repeated his proposal in her presence, and again grandfather insisted that Henry should remain at the Glebe. Thereupon Kate fixed her brother with her sharp little eyes. 'Ned!' she said. 'Get the boy in!' So he was brought in and Kate looked him up and down as if in astonishment.

'Well!' she said. 'What have we here? My father couldn't be rid of us fast enough. Bessie to Greece, me to America, Polly to Chesterfield, your father to Hedingham, and Pat to God knows where in London! All pushed out or given away! And your father won't let you go. Aren't you grateful?'

'Yes, Aunt Kate,' said Henry untruthfully.

'Then you're a fool, my boy. Fathers throw you out if it suits them, and they keep you if it suits them. Fathers, like everyone else, think only of number one. And you're old enough to do the same.'

'Yes, Aunt Kate,' said Henry with more conviction.

117

'Well then, what do you want? To go with your uncle, or to stay with your father?'

'To go with my uncle, Aunt Kate.'

'You're quite sure?'

'Yes, Aunt Kate.'

'Then leave us while your father and I have a talk.'

Henry was dismissed, and Charlie also withdrew to save his cousin's face. Grandfather and his sister were locked in combat for nearly an hour, and voices were raised. What changed his mind was never known for certain, but no one in the family had any doubt that Kate finally turned the financial screw. Grandfather had borrowed from her to tide over a bad harvest and was not yet able to repay. He might again need her help in a poor season, and Kate was known to be ruthless to those who displeased her. 'Henry,' he said when they emerged, 'you can go to your uncle.' That was all. Grandfather accepted life as it came, because there was nothing else to do. He bore no resentment against Kate, Charlie, or Henry. Farmers were used to late frosts and storms in August, and no family was fed by complaining. He had lost, like a crop, the son he had intended to succeed to the five hundred freehold acres that were his relentless ambition. Henry would have been a bigger farmer than any Anderson or Kirby. He would have sat on the top of the Hedingham heap. Grandfather now had to make do with James, the next best, so he took himself off into his fields to find fault with the way his second choice was plashing the hedges.

When Henry moved into the cobbler's house, he was given Louisa's room and she had to sleep in the same room as Sarah Bell, the maid. This is some indication of Uncle Charlie's affection for his nephew, because the new sleeping arrangements made it impossible for him any longer to slip into Sarah's bed when on fine nights his wife was out in the summerhouse. Nor could Sarah leave her room to join Uncle Charlie unless she was certain that the curious Louisa was soundly asleep. Nevertheless Charlie put up with these inconveniences gladly enough, and Louisa would have shared a bedroom with a dozen maids if that were the price of having Henry in the same house. Though still only ten she already adored her cousin and was determined to be his wife. Her father was of the same mind. Even if he could not have Henry as his adopted son, he would have him as his son-in-law. So the overt long-term plan was that Henry should in due course marry Louisa. The plan went awry because, although Louisa remained constant, Henry found that several years of living under the same roof with her only laid the foundation for a quite invincible dislike. However, he had the good sense to realize that his bread was buttered on the side of leaving both Louisa and his uncle with grounds for hope as long as he possibly could.

The terms of Henry's employment were that he should work from seven to midday in Charlie's garden for six shillings a week, and devote the afternoons to study. His uncle provided books, paper, tutorials, discussions, arguments, criticism, oral examinations and encouragement. By the time he left Hedingham Henry was highly educated, though it was not the education of a gentleman. Of Latin and Greek he was as ignorant as a cow, and he knew as little of the history of the Punic Wars as he did of the Expedition of the Ten Thousand; but he was pushed right into the heart of the intellectual ferment of Victorian England. While boys at Eton and Winchester were construing Greek and composing Latin verses, Henry was wrestling with Bagehot's *Physics and Politics*, Spencer's *Principles of Biology*, Robert Chambers's *Vestiges of Creation*, Darwin's *The Origin of Species*, Lyell's *The Principles of Geology*, Herschel's *Physical Geography of the Globe*, Thomas Huxley's *Man's Place in Nature*, Francis Galton's *Hereditary Genius*, Maine's *Ancient Law*, William Stubbs's *Constitutional History of England*, Henry Buckle's *Introduction to the History of Civilization in England*, Tylor's *Researches in the Early History of Mankind*, Bentham's *Introduction to the Principles of Morals and Legislation*, Adam Smith's *Wealth of Nations*, Hobbes's *Leviathan*, Locke's *Essay Concerning Human Understanding*, J. S. Mill's *On Liberty*. Those are only some of the books I can remember seeing on Uncle Charlie's bookshelves. In German he had David Strauss's *Leben Jesu*, Goethe's *Faust*, and *Leiden des jungen Werthers*, and works by Hegel, Kant, and Nietzsche. In French there were Pascal, Rousseau and Voltaire. Henry told me that by the time he was seventeen he had read all the books in English in his uncle's house, and was struggling with the French and German. It was heavy intellectual fodder for a boy in his teens. If Henry's temperament had been less gay and light-hearted he might have been weighed down by it, because his uncle was not conspicuous in the family for his levity. He pursued knowledge with a devoted respect that would have commended itself to a High Master of Manchester Grammar School, and he gathered together a small fortune with the sobriety of a Quaker. In the eighteen nineties Uncle Charlie was still a serious-minded Victorian untouched, like the Queen, by the crumbling of the structure that became an Edwardian landslide. Even his adultery with Sarah Bell was the satisfaction of a reasonable human need. It was not a cheerful wickedness.

Henry used to say that his Uncle Charlie understood what his bookshelves had taught him, but failed to draw the right conclusions. Galileo had deprived the earth of its celestial significance. Darwin had put man in his place within creation. Bentham had demonstrated benevolence to be a sensible self-interested aid to survival. Locke had reduced metaphysics to futility. Hobbes had dethroned justice, and buried free will. Uncle Charlie was well aware of all that, and was also a bee-keeper. He was intelligent enough to see our society within the context of all societies, whether of bees, ants, salmon or lemmings. The brute creation had evolved one way and we another. The differences between human and other civilizations were enormous in kind, but not in essence. We were as cruel, devoted, selfish, altruistic and as determined in our habits as they. And all to no purpose beyond the temporary survival of the species until some galactic catastrophe put it beyond the reach even of chance mutation.

Charlie Rudkin lived with this knowledge as if he were still in ignorance, either with the momentum of his upbringing or because he thought there was nothing else to do. But Henry, after being appalled by the realities of existence, threw himself deliberately into the business of making the best of it. After all, the doomed husband of the black widow had his moment of ecstasy. The worker bee flew avid with desire to the sprays of nectar-laden honeysuckle. The poor drone strained, desperate with lust, up ever higher into the sky in pursuit of his queen, even if later he was to be turned out of the hive in winter to starve. All creation, at times, enjoyed existence, and so would he. Within the human species it was very apparent that some enjoyed more than others their brief appearance between nothing and nothing. The moral for Henry was obvious. He must join the fortunate few. He parted company from the Benthamites, being unconcerned with the greatest happiness for the greatest number. He made a self-conscious resolve to be concerned with his own, not in any crude sense that might be thought, wrongly, to be epicurean; but by a calculated balancing of present and future advantages, and a careful pursuit of optimum reward. Uncle Charlie had a translation of *The Odyssey* that became Henry's bible. There he found that bronze-age Greeks had perfectly understood the human predicament, though in terms remote from the cold reasoning of Darwin and Malthus. For them there was no benevolent deity, but a group of feckless and cruel godlings who had the human race at their mercy. There was no source of reliable and consistent help. If things went well it behoved a Greek to look out for disaster. Fortune and misfortune could succeed each other without rhyme or reason. Reward was as likely to follow vice as virtue. Yet far from discouraged, the Greeks had developed their extraordinary zest for life. Odysseus of the hyacinthine locks became Henry's ideal man. Like him he would out-face the callous universe with strength and cunning, or fail with dignity.

Even so, further relief from the weight of Uncle Charlie's

bookshelves was on its way. He had a friend, Rory Tod-
hunter, who was a farmer in a distant village but who rode
over occasionally to play chess. On one occasion he found
Henry reading Herbert Spencer. 'God Almighty, boy!' he
said. 'You'll drive yourself mad with that stuff. All brains
and no guts!' Then he had a prowl round his friend's
library, though he knew very well what it contained, tut-
tutting as he went and asking when he was going to find
the tits and bottoms and the good dinners. After a very dis-
paraging tour he sank into a chair, and sighed deeply. 'Well,
well!' he said. 'I knew your blood was pretty thin, Charlie,
but I'd no idea you were making that boy anaemic as well.
Where's the red meat? And where are my old friends?
Where are all the drinkers and fornicators?' At that Charlie
could do no more than raise a wan smile. 'I suppose you
wouldn't mind,' Rory went on, 'if I educated the poor lad
a bit myself, would you?' Charlie shook his head, so Rory
promised that on his next visit he would bring Henry the
very thing he needed. What he brought was his own beloved
dog-eared copy of Rabelais, in Urquhart's translation. He
handed it over : 'There, boy, that will blow some of the dust
of Kant and Hegel out of your eyes, and raise the sap in your
nether parts. And when you've done with this, there's
always Sterne, Smollett and Fielding to keep your thoughts
off the Utilitarians while you lie in bed at night clutching
your starved manhood. They all learned something from
this randy old doctor of French physic. And so can you.'
In fact, the next chapter will show that Henry's young manhood was far from starved. All that Rabelais and the others
did for him was to provide an agreeable literary background
to his amorous adventures until he came later to meet ladies
of cultural pretensions. Then he found that an apt quotation
afforded from time to time a useful lever for rolling them
into bed.

Until Henry's voice broke he continued to sing to the Squire's daughter, but puberty ruptured his only means of communication. Thereafter he attended mattins to stare at Nancy's back and occasionally to catch her eye as the Pitt-Melvilles filed down the nave out of church while the rest of the congregation waited respectfully in their pews. But that was all he saw of her, except by chance as she rode through the village. It was poor nourishment for an adolescent passion, and by the time he was fifteen Henry's church-going had almost ceased. A stronger faith than his might have sustained hopes of felicity, but there seemed to him no chance of ever being able to exchange even a word with his beloved. Desperate thoughts of climbing like Romeo to her bedroom were idle because the Hall servants reported that Nancy still shared a room with her governess. 'Oh why?' Henry asked his Uncle Charlie in exasperation. 'Why do the gentry never allow their daughters to be alone for one moment?' It was a cry of frustration, not an inquiry. He knew the answer well enough: 'Because of men like you.' However, the dark Anderson twins continued, now separately, to be kissed and fumbled, but they were not disposed to surrender all to importunities that each knew to be directed impartially towards the other. Henry was not experienced enough to know that even a feigned preference for one might have secured both. So it fell to Mrs William Anderson, a few days before his sixteenth birthday, to be the first with whom he made love. She was twenty-five and the wife of the Hedingham miller. She was also, of course, my grandfather's cousin, but the relationship only started there and continued in bed. Furthermore Mrs William was, to use one of my grandmother's euphemisms, 'gracious' to several other husbands in the village as well, because her greatest pride, after her little spinet with ivory keys, was her beautiful and hospitable body. For all that, Mrs William was one of my grandmother's closest friends because she was astringent and witty, and grandmother always preferred to be entertained by the wicked than bored by the righteous. On the other hand, my Aunt Matilda was less tolerant of transgression. She described her in an extraordinary confusion of metaphor as a 'lily'—a flower then enjoying some pre-Raphaelite notoriety—'with the tongue of a viper'.

Only one of Mrs William's caustic remarks has survived. She called upon my grandmother one morning and was shown by the maid into the sitting-room. Grandmother had been cooking, so when she came in she said, 'How nice to see you, Mrs William! But would you mind waiting while I go upstairs to make myself beautiful?' 'Oh, in that case', her visitor replied, rising from her chair, 'I will bid you good-day!' However, Mrs William was kind to Henry, and on many afternoons when they were supposed to be playing together on the violin and spinet, on which she was only an indifferent performer, they were better occupied in the miller's feather bed, which was stuffed with the softest and finest down from the bellies and hindquarters of chickens, ducks and geese. The voluptuousness of those rural mattresses was incomparable. 'No man has known true bliss,' my Uncle Henry told me, 'unless he has slept with a loving woman in a feather bed.' If I say that Mrs William Anderson taught Henry the art of love, I wish not to be misunderstood. From her he learned no improbable contortions. She was a sensualist, not a gymnast. She taught the simple do's and don'ts of affectionate human intercourse. Being as well balanced as the action of a wrist watch, the miller's wife did not hanker after outlandish practices. For her there was no joy in pain. A long slow trailing of delicate fingers was her delight. Her kisses were gentle and infinitely prolonged, at times a mere brushing of lips, at others a subtle conversation between the very tips of tongues. 'Rough impatient men I abhor,' said Mrs William. 'I share with the Bible a dislike of unruly members. Restraint, my dear boy, is the secret of making love.' Whether she was right or not, going to bed with her was a good discipline: 'Don't hurry, boy! You're not riding a horse in the Lincolnshire Handicap.' Or again: 'Henry! If I wanted to be bitten, I'd made love out in the woods.' Thus he was instructed by a lady with firm opinions and the ability to express them with force and economy.

Henry now cast about to practise his skills with a younger relative, or even outside the family altogether. Unfortunately, his eldest brother John tended, with his remarkable good looks, to dominate the field. To attract women Henry had first to be able to engage them in conversation, whereas John had only to be seen to be desired. Though moderate in his needs, it was difficult to find a pretty and complaisant girl in Hedingham with whom John had not made love, and still more difficult to find one there who had also escaped the notice of his father. Henry was too fastidious to play jackal to that pair of lions, so he turned his attention to the Kirby household in Snitterby, while continuing to carry his violin weekly to the miller's house. The Kirby's had no young daughter, but a distant relative, a little orphan girl called Rebecca, lived with them as a dependent. Occasionally Henry was invited to their house, and he soon captivated Rebecca by his talk which, while appearing to be general, was really directed at her. She was not beautiful because her nose was a little too short and her mouth was a little too wide, but she had large pale blue eyes and straight flaxen hair, a legacy of the Danish invasions. She was only just fifteen, small built and small boned with little round breasts and the most enchanting limbs. Her delicate thighs narrowed into tiny knees, and then came a gentle crescendo in the calves, subsiding again into slender ankles and long thin feet. Henry pursued her relentlessly and the poor child fell in love with him. Yet for months and months she resisted, allowing only kisses and caresses, until the very tenderness that Mrs Anderson had taught him was the girl's undoing. Rebecca mistook it for love. One long warm evening in the corner of a hay field this little virgin waif submitted, only to be so mortified and ashamed that she would never thereafter be alone with her seducer. There was a great deal of immorality in north Lincolnshire, but some girls were virtuous and Rebecca was one of them. My mother was another, and she thoroughly disapproved of her brother Henry. I have said that the family loved him, and in one sense they did. People responded to him at two levels. Few could resist his charm and gaiety. Even my mother was fond enough of him to call her second son Henry; but not the first. She had reservations, and so had others : they sensed the hard core of selfishness that had chosen Rebecca as his victim.

I have weighted this book with the sad story of Rebecca from a sense of male guilt. Most men, at one time or another, have taken advantage of women. Who can hear Dido's Lament, above Purcell's disquieting ground bass, without being moved to shame for mankind? So I turn with relief to my Aunt Charlotte who brought not only Henry but my grandfather and three of his other sons to an absolute nonplus. She was a Chesterfield Maitland, the daughter of James who had put Aunt Polly into the workhouse. He owned a large house in Saltergate and never kept less than three maids. James and his wife Tabitha lived in great style. According to my Aunt Matilda, the Chesterfield Maitlands were 'as big as bull beef'. My grandfather went to see them, and reported that 'even a rasher of bacon' was borne into the dining-room on a silver dish under a silver lid by a correctly dressed parlourmaid. At the top of the house were the day and night nurseries and when, long after James's death, Aunt Matilda was invited to Chesterfield she found the nursery suite exactly as it had been for the children because 'Mama and Papa would have liked it so'. Aunt Kate, who loathed James Maitland, had been obliged to concede that he 'looked like a nobleman'; but my grandfather was not so impressed by the air of pale distinction and described him less charitably as 'a walking corpse'. Nevertheless he sired many children who were brought up with nursemaids and governesses, French and piano lessons. He had three sons, and of his five daughters only two married. Fanny, Lily and Charlotte remained spinsters. Fanny was 'a brisk little gentlewoman' and played the piano extremely well. I remember Lily in her old age. Her skin was wrinkled as if her face had been too long in soak. She had a shock of white hair that never thinned, a soft gentle voice and perfect manners. She played the piano almost as well as the brisk gentlewoman. Charlotte, with whom we are more concerned, had the drip-white skin of the Maitland family, a long narrow nose, a small mouth and brown limpid eyes. Her dark hair was drawn straight back from her face into a big bun at the back of her head. She was tall and thin with narrow shoulders, and since her head was small and she wore long wide skirts, she presented the general outline of a triangle with its base sweeping the ground, as she glided rather than walked in her long button boots.

Charlotte was twenty-seven when she first visited the Glebe. She delighted my grandmother with her ability to play the piano for hours on end with great fluency and from memory. Her repertoire consisted of 'The War March of the Priests', 'Robin's Return', 'Poet and Peasant', 'Maiden's Prayer', 'Christ and His Soldiers', the overture to *Zampa* and other pieces of that kind. This was the music that my grandmother loved, and my mother never lost her taste for similar rubbish after her early exposure to it. Cousin Charlotte, being so carefully nurtured, could be expected to play the piano; but nothing in her appearance, nor in her Chesterfield background, had prepared Matilda for the shock of looking by chance out of the kitchen window to see her father in the orchard with Charlotte lying beneath him. Her long black skirt was round her neck and there was everywhere a flurry of petticoats. Even at that distance Matilda could hear through the open window the sound of subdued cursing as if her father were in difficulties. Matilda immediately averted her gaze, but after a few days the astonishing news began to circulate. Cousin Charlotte was still a virgin. The attempt witnessed by Matilda had been grandfather's last. He had admitted defeat. The family were incredulous. Nothing like that had ever happened before, and grandfather was still in the prime of life. So reinforcements poured into what ought to have been the breach, but only to restore his reputation. John, James and Henry were equally unsuccessful. Each failed miserably, and all now depended on Robert, who was only twelve and thin. Perhaps he might find some small gap in the defences. But no. Years later he summed up for me the family's predicament: 'Cousin Charlotte Maitland was so small underneath that you couldn't have got the end of a lead pencil in.' Then he allowed himself a modest boast, 'But she told me that I gave her the worst time of all.' That was said in a very limited context, because Charlotte left the Glebe well pleased with her stay. When my mother visited Chesterfield as a young woman, Charlotte showed her two little hazel nuts gathered from the tree shading the lawn at Hedingham. She had kept them as a memento of 'the happiest time I ever had in my life'. Perhaps my unfortunate aunt was simply grateful for the concern that had been shown, and the resources that had been deployed, in an endeavour that was often repeated, but for ever remained hopeless.

If Cousin Charlotte enjoyed her visit, she was equally appreciated as a guest. My grandmother once explained to me why Charlotte was so acceptable. She had beautiful manners. She was never known to feel unwell nor to mention an ailment. To every request the answer was, 'Certainly,

128

cousin!' 'Charlotte! Will you play to us?' 'Charlotte! Will you have a game of cards?' 'Will you take Fluff' (the Pomeranian) 'for a walk?' 'Would you post our letters?' 'Will you help us pick currants?' 'Would you like to go to church?' Always came the reply, 'Why certainly, cousin!' Nevertheless, Charlotte was one of the many who came to stay at the Glebe but were not within the inner circle of relatives invited to the formal annual gathering of the family on New Year's Day. It was not held then on account of Robert Maitland's supposed Scottish ancestry, but because it was my grandparents' wedding anniversary. Every year on the first of January my grandmother took great trouble to demonstrate that her marriage to Edward Fisher was worth celebrating. Aunt Kate usually arranged to be home from America, although she was given neither to parties nor to matrimony. My great-aunts Pat and Polly walked across the Green to be reminded of what they had both missed. Polly had no strong feelings about the occasion, being too dull of intellect even to add up the disadvantages of spinsterhood; but Pat was saddened by the New Year's parties, while maintaining a spark in her eye: 'I love children and I love men,' she said, 'but of the former I've had none, and of the latter too many.' The others who came were all married—Uncle Charlie and Aunt Rudkin, Uncle Joseph and Aunt Hiles, and various Atkinsons, Andersons and Kirbys. Whether they liked to be reminded of weddings was immaterial, because grandmother provided enough food and drink to have distracted attention from the reality of a funeral.

The dining-room table was laden with a stuffed chine, pork pies, haslets, ham and chicken. Then there were jam tarts, lemon curd tarts, cheesecakes, plum bread, red American cheese and apple pie. The men drank whisky, or beer from a barrel that was kept in a dark cupboard under the stairs. Grandfather himself undertook the tricky job of hammering the bung and immediately pushing in the spigot and tap with as little loss of beer as possible. Matilda, as his favourite daughter, was always enlisted as assistant to hold the candle, and she was always unable to do it to his satis-faction. The women guests were provided with home-made cowslip, dandelion, parsnip and elderberry wine or, if they had a taste for spirits, with sloe gin and cherry brandy. Uncle Joseph, however, would drink nothing alcoholic because he had signed the pledge ; but by a merciful dispen-sation, port wine was regarded in Nonconformist circles as a medicinal tonic. It was freely prescribed by Dr Rainbird for those suffering from religious melancholy to lift them into a state of mild intoxication indistinguishable from beatitude. So Uncle Joseph had his special bottle of ruby port, and Aunt Hiles as a dutiful wife shared it with him. Conversa-tion was the main entertainment of the evening because most of the guests, except Aunt Kate, loved talking, but at some stage in the evening my grandmother would be per-suaded to recite Tennyson's 'Northern Farmer' in the authen-tic dialect of her childhood. I heard it many times, but always under the name of the 'Lincolnshire Farmer'. Tennyson had been brought up in Somersby, not many miles away, and educated at Louth Grammar School. We had no doubt about the origin of the poem. It came from Lincolnshire, and the farmer who admonishes his lovesick son as they ride together might have been one of the family. The boy wants to marry the daughter of a parson who is 'nobbut a curate', so she's a hopeless proposition :

Parson's lass 'ant nowt, an' weän't 'a nowt when 'e's deäd,
Mun be a guvness, lad, or summut, and addle her breäd.

Grandmother recited the whole of the poem from memory, but as it is rather long, I will set out only some of the more apposite verses :

Dosn't thou 'ear my 'erse's legs, as they canters awaäy?
Proputty, proputty, proputty—that's what I 'ears 'em saäy.
Proputty, proputty, proputty—Sam, thou's an ass for they
   paäins :
Theer's more sense i' one o' 'is legs nor in all thy braäins...

Me an' thy muther, Sammy, 'as beän a-talkin' o' thee ;
Thou's beän talkin' to muther, an' she beän a-tellin' it me.
Thou'll not marry for munny—thou's sweet upo' parson's
  lass—
Noä—thou'll marry fur luvv—an' we boäth on us thinks
  tha an ass ! . . .

Do'ant be stunt : taäke time : I knaws what maäkes tha
  sa mad.
Warn't I craäzed fur the lasses mysén when I wur a lad?
But I knaw'd a Quaäker feller as often 'as towd ma this :
'Doänt thou marry for munny, but goä wheer munny is !'

An' I went wheer munny war ; an' they muther coom to
  'and,
Wi' lots o' munny laäid by, an' a nicetish bit o' land.
Maäybe she warn't a beauty :—I never giv it a thowt—
But warn't she as good to cuddle an' kiss as a lass as 'ant
  nowt? . . .

Luvv? what's luvv? thou can luvv thy lass an' 'er munny
  too,
Maäkin' 'em goa togither as they've good right to do.
Could'n I luvv thy muther by cause o' 'er munny laäid by?
Naäy—fur I luvv'd 'er a vast sight moor fur it : reäson
  why . . .

'Tis'n them as 'as munny as breäks into 'ouses an' steäls,
Them as 'as coäts to their backs an' taäkes their regular
  meäls.
Noä, but it's them as niver knaws wheer a meäl's to be 'ad.
Taäke my word for it, Sammy, the poor in a loomp is bad.

Them or thir feythers, tha sees, mun 'a beän a laäzy lot,
Fur work mun a' gone to the gittin' whiniver munny was
  got.
Feyther 'ad ammost nowt ; leastways 'is munny was 'id.
But 'e tued an' moil'd 'issén deäd, an' 'e died a good un,
  'e did.

Loök thou theer wheer Wrigglesby beck cooms out by
the 'ill !
Feyther run oop to the farm, an' I runs oop to the mill ;
An' I'll run oop to the brig, an' that thou'll live to see ;
And if thou marries a good un I'll leäve the land to thee.

Thim's my noätions, Sammy, wheerby I means to stick ;
But if thou marries a bad un, I'll leäve the land to Dick—
Coom oop, proputty, proputty—that's what I 'ears 'im
saäy—
Proputty, proputty, proputty—canter an' canter awaäy.

Grandmother recited that version of the 'Northern
Farmer' at family gatherings right up to the age of ninety.
If pressed, she would follow it with the 'Old Style' version
which was in a stronger dialect and more difficult to understand. In this poem the old farmer is on his death-bed, complaining of his nurse, his doctor, and the parson : 'An' a
towd me ma sins an's toithe were due . . .' He even chides
the Almighty for taking the wrong man and at the wrong
time in the agricultural cycle :

A mowt 'a taäen owd Joänes, as 'ant not a aäpoth o' sense,
Or a mowt 'a taäen young Robins—a niver mended a
fence :
But godamoighty a moost taäke meä an' taäke ma now
Wi' aaf the cows to cauve, an' Thurnaby hoäms to plow !

The 'Northern Farmer' was closer to the centre of Tennyson's personality than much of his other poetry, like *Idylls
of the King*, that was produced for the Victorian market. As
a man he was almost as earthy as his Lincolnshire background. There is a story of him, ennobled and famous, being
the lion at a county garden party. He soon wearied of the
fulsome adulation and took himself off alone to a remote
summerhouse where he found, to his annoyance, a timid
girl also sheltering from the other guests. Having fled from
the less distinguished, she was horrified to find herself alone

with the great man himself, with his large black cloak, his wide-brimmed hat and his craggy features. Not daring to make her departure, she waited trembling with fear for him to open the conversation; but for several minutes he only stared at her, increasing her nervousness to desperation. Then at last he broke the silence: 'Your stays are creaking!' At this the poor girl could only take to her heels and leave the Poet Laureate in peace.

Grandmother's performance at the New Year's party, though well received, was not the highlight of the evening. A clockmaker from Gainsborough provided that with his comic songs. Charlie Clay was so expert in his trade that he could say whether the grandfather clock at the Glebe was running fast or slow by listening to the tick. He was also a very talented entertainer, and was invited to the party for that reason, although he could claim a tenuous relationship with the family because his wife, like Charlie Rudkin's mother, was one of the formidable Uttings. Charlie Clay's expertise with clocks did not extend to his business affairs, and there came a time when he realized that he could no longer meet his debts, so he asked a solicitor to file his petition in bankruptcy. When Charlie outlined his financial difficulties and explained how he had approached all his friends and acquaintances for loans without success, the solicitor listened with amazement. He knew that Charlie had married one of his clients, a Miss Utting, and had, moreover, married her before the Married Women's Property Act became law. So her property was his. He also knew that Miss Utting had many hundreds of pounds. The solicitor knew more than Charlie, for his wife had kept him in ignorance that she had any money at all. The shock of realizing that his life's partner had sat by silent while he was searching desperately for financial help, so upset poor Charlie Clay that he had a nervous breakdown. As usual, my Aunt Matilda put it more plainly: 'For about three months he went off his head.' The solicitor told Mrs Clay that she must meet her husband's debts, because her money was legally his, and the creditors could sue for it. So when Charlie recovered his composure, he found his clock-making business free from debt and in better financial shape, through his wife's attentions, than it had ever been. Mrs Clay ensured that it so continued. Thereafter she ran the business and he made the clocks.

When the time came for Charlie Clay to perform at the New Year's party, all the guests squeezed into the living-room, some moving from the sitting-room, others from the kitchen, where they had congregated in small groups to play chess, or to play cards, or to talk. Charlie sat down at the piano waiting for everyone to settle into silence. He was small and thin, except that between the wings of his open fustian jacket there was an enormous expanse of check waistcoat. It was remarkable that anyone so spare in face, arms and legs, could have so huge a paunch. Across the acres of waistcoat was a heavy gold watch-chain hung pro-fusely with bundles of seals and gold medallions. He was entirely bald, apart from tufts of light brown hair over his ears and extending backwards round the lower part of his head, but the high pink dome of his skull was comple-mented by a pointed imperial beard, in the fashion of the Prince of Wales. Between these two extremities was a pale oval face dominated by a pair of large gold-rimmed spec-tacles. Charlie Clay was so short-sighted that the thick lenses showed concentric circles diminishing in diameter and receding, apparently, into the very back of his head where, as if at the end of a tunnel, twinkled two distant eyes, intensely blue, but reduced in size by the lenses to those of a fieldmouse.

All preparations completed and the audience assembled, Charlie moved the stool as close to the piano as his stomach allowed and had a preliminary canter over the keyboard by way of a series of brilliant runs, arpeggios, trills and appog-giaturas, all improvised and played with tremendous panache, cascading from one end of the keyboard to the other. Eventually the torrent of notes began to settle into one definite key, and Charlie leaned back on the piano stool, lifted his eyes to the ceiling, opened his mouth, and began to sing in a light tenor. Most of his songs were about the perils of matrimony, but strain my memory as I will, I can remember the names of only three of them—'My Wife's Relations', 'Leeds Owd Church' and 'The Black Pudding'. Charlie's repertoire was in fact very large, but he was never at a loss for the music because he played by ear. Sometimes, however, he needed to be reminded of the words, so he carried in his pocket a few grubby pieces of paper to which he referred at intervals. As he warmed to his themes, Charlie's eyes darted about amongst the audience in delight. He rolled in mirth around the circumference of the piano stool, his beard wagging and his arms performing the most extraordinary arabesques. For him there was no thumping of a few stale chords as an accompaniment. Every song had its own particular setting—mocking trills, thuds of derision, menacing runs down to the lower registers when disaster impended, light-hearted runs upwards when all was well again, and always air, buoyancy and bravura in the playing. Yet the piano never drowned the clarity of the words. The tempo varied constantly. At very dramatic moments in the recitals Charlie stopped playing altogether, only to resume with long intricate cadenzas to hold everyone on edge waiting for the happy dénouement when the theme galloped joyfully away again. Year after year the same songs were repeated, and year after year the family were falling about helpless with merriment—with two exceptions. Aunt Kate pretended to be a little amused, and Charlie's wife, the former Miss Utting, sat silent, impassive and disapproving.

A familiar character from an earlier part of this book, the lovely Bridget Atkinson, was always among the guests. Now Mrs George Anderson and a mature matron, she was still placid and charming. The softness of the face the Rector had loved was gone, replaced by a taut angularity that made her more beautiful, because her bones were fine and delicate, but less desirable. Only her gentle brown eyes were preserved from the snatch of time. They reflected a mellow content that my grandfather, in his male arrogance, attributed to her early years of being well loved at the Rectory. 'That parson knows his business,' he used to say, 'you can read it in all their eyes.' In fact, Bridget was doe-like by nature, and fortunately so, because George Anderson was not an ideal husband. With her dowry of two hundred pounds he had set up as a builder and prospered on the wages of the Rector's sin; but after many years of matrimony he fell in love with a young girl and took her away to Nottingham. There he rented a house and lived for a year in idleness and concupiscence, leaving the building business to be managed by his foreman. Then, tiring of the girl, he forsook her and returned unannounced late one night to the arms of his forgiving wife. The next morning George rose early and went to the farm where his workmen were building a barn. He stood on the site, watch in hand, to see if any of his men arrived after six. One of them was two minutes late, and the first words he heard from his master, after a twelve-month truancy, were, 'If you're going to go on working for me, you'll have to start a bit earlier, work a bit faster, and stay a bit longer.'

At the New Year my grandmother's father, old Thomas Millson, abandoned his usual bedtime of nine o'clock. He abandoned even his bowl of bread and milk, and concentrated on the whisky. He had never drunk regularly or heavily, but he loved at intervals to be tipsy. When he was the Redbourne blacksmith he walked once a week to Brigg for a night in the public houses. Now with age, and his daughter to admonish him, he was restricted to an occasional party at the Glebe. But when Brigg Fair was on Thomas would walk over to see his friend Isaac Spike for a plate of cold beef and cold ham, washed down with pints of beer and glasses of gin. Then they went to the fair. One day they found a teetotaller exhorting the people to sign the pledge. Old Isaac, who was eighty, listened for a while and then broke in: ''Ow oald a ta?' The speaker said that he was thirty-five, and Isaac went on, 'A've sooped oop a bottle o' geen hevery daa o' me loif, an' I dusne luke a daa owlda' ne thee!' Thomas was also helped by alcohol to forget his years. At a New Year party it induced him to conceive that he might still be loved by a young woman, and his attentions to Mrs William Anderson, the beautiful wife of the Heding-ham miller, provoked my grandmother to ask, 'Father? Isn't it time you went to bed?' 'Aye, bairn,' he replied, 'so long as this one goes up with me!' 'Now, Mr Millson,' interposed Mrs William, 'we know perfectly well that with you in your condition it would be a useless journey.' Thomas shook his head sadly : 'Pity 'tis you're right, love, for you're a fine woman. But time was when I could've made you squeal !' His son Tom was better behaved, having sobering responsibilities at home. He came from Grays in Essex, where he lived with a woman called Harriet, who had deserted her husband in favour of unholy matrimony with Tom. She could not re-marry because she was never divorced. Harriet brought several children by her first hus-band, and not content with that she bred extensively with Tom. They had ten more, but almost all of them were con-sumed by tuberculosis.

Tom Millson was old Thomas's only surviving son. His first boy James, my grandmother's beloved brother Jim, was clever and became a compositor in Gainsborough until consumption killed him when he was a little over twenty. The last thing he wanted on earth was pigeon pie but, between the request and the cooking of it, he expired. The other son Tom was, in my grandmother's opinion, a 'blob-head' in comparison. His father trained him as a blacksmith, and this enabled him to find work as a ship repairer in Grays in the Port of London. Tom was not so stupid as my grandmother, in loyalty to Jim, who made out because he progressed from manual work to become a supervisor. My mother said that he was 'a smart, shrewd-looking man—and perhaps dishonest'. She added the rider because he loved gambling, of which she disapproved, and had acquired from his close acquaintance with the sea and ships the slightly raffish air of a sailor. He also acquired from the sailors enough parrots to supply the Glebe with a surfeit of them. He would arrive with one of these birds on his arm, and in politeness it had to be accepted. No one wanted a parrot. The children hated them, and would never feed them willingly nor clean their cages. My grandmother, who was a bird lover, was at best a parrot tolerator. The first was a roselle—small and red, with a long tail. It behaved exceptionally only in the manner of its dying. Suddenly, after eating cucumber, it started to spin round its cage, and expired in a fit. Another was a white cockatoo with a pink head. In spite of the supposed longevity of parrots, there seemed never to be more than one at the Glebe at a time, although Tom Millson even sent a reinforcement by train. It arrived at Kirton station in a wooden box and as it stood waiting on the platform to be collected, an inquisitive man peered into the box, to be greeted with 'Hello!' in a deep sepulchral voice. This one was grey, with a red tail, and 'Go to school!' was the favourite item in his repertory. My Uncle George used to tell of how he and his brother Robert grew sick of being thus admonished and sewed up the parrot's behind. Why closing that aperture should be expected to stop it talking is difficult to understand and points, like the sequel, to the apocryphal nature of the anecdote. The operation was wholly unsuccessful because the bird was able indignantly to denounce the offenders by reporting, 'Robert held while Georgie sewed.'

In spite of the parrots, the children loved Tom Millson's frequent visits to the Glebe. He never tired of entertaining them with his talk and, having fine beautiful hands, he was an expert conjurer. Tom was fond of children, but he had enough at home, so that was not what drew him to Hedingham so often. My grandfather knew well enough what it was. Tom used to spend hours looking lovingly upon the names 'Thomas Millson and E. M. Fisher' painted on the farm carts. He was old Thomas's only son and heir and expected to inherit a half-share of the farm, but when his father died several years later Tom found that he had been circumvented. As ever, Charlie Rudkin had a hand in it.

In 1867 Parliament extended the county franchise to males
with leaseholds and copyholds of five pounds and to occu-
piers of twelve pounds rateable value. Even Disraeli, who
introduced the Bill, called it 'a leap in the dark'; but
Coventry Patmore was in no doubt about the consequences.
1867 marked the end of the power of the aristocracy, so he
uttered his cry of anguish:

> In the year of the great crime
> When the false English Nobles and their Jew,
> By God demented, slew
> The trust they stood twice pledged to keep from
>   wrong . . .

The great crime enfranchised my grandfather and Uncle
Charlie, with others of the middle classes. The Liberal
bourgeoisie might then have thanked God for dementing
the nobles and rested content with their new-found power,
but instead they made it their party policy to extend the
franchise further to the remaining ninety per cent of the adult

male population. Looking back, it seems strange that Victorian Liberals should seek to ice the national cake with political benevolence while expecting to cut it afterwards in much the same shares as before. Yet they did. Although Charlie Rudkin's library was packed with evidence that power of one kind or another determines the fate of every variety and species in creation, he was incapable of seeing that if political power were given to journeymen and labourers, they would in the nature of things turn it against their masters. Charlie and my grandfather worked assiduously for reform without the least intention that their enfranchised workmen should become significantly less submissive and manageable, nor that labourers' daughters should cease to be had for a pittance as servant girls and mistresses. Perhaps it was the short-term advantages of being an active Liberal that closed their minds to an understanding that they were laying the foundations for a society they did not want, and would have detested. The immediate advantages for Uncle Charlie were real. The Tories would never have made him a Justice of the Peace, but the Liberals did. The County Association nominated him as one of their quota of magistrates shortly before Henry went to live at the cobbler's shop. This lifted the village bootmaker several rungs up the Hedingham ladder, and made him beyond question the most distinguished member of the family. Until then we had sometimes appeared before the bench, but never sat upon it. So Liberalism had its present rewards, while sowing dragons' teeth for the future.

Characteristically, even before he was sworn in, Charlie went to Lincoln to order the latest editions of the most erudite treatises on the criminal law, such as Archbold's *Criminal Pleading and Practice*, *Phipson on Evidence*, and *Mayhew on Mayhem*. Before long he knew more about the law of *animus furandi* than the Clerk to the Justices himself, which was not difficult. Ronald James Arthur Ponsonby, M.A. (Oxon.), was the senior partner in a Kirton practice so long established that he did not deign to screw a brass plate on to the door of the Georgian house to which clients had found their way unaided for more than a century. Generations of his family had been legal flunkeys to the Hutton-Palethorpes who administered justice in that part of the country. Sir Hugh, the fourth baronet and Chairman of the Bench, was accustomed to fine and jail the local malefactors with a discretion unfettered by objection or dissent from his fellow magistrates. Nor was he much inclined to hearken unto the evidence before forming his judgments. Prior to going into court he ran a finger down the cause list to see what he could find. 'Ah yes, Ponsonby,' Sir Hugh would say, 'know that fellow! Known him all his life. Needs a good stiff fine. Good stiff fine.' Perhaps Ponsonby would then draw attention to one his Chairman had missed: 'Seen that chap before, haven't we?' 'By God, you're right, Ponsonby! Taken more pheasant off me than I care to remember. High time he went down!' In court the word of a gamekeeper was more persuasive than Holy Writ. After one of them had given evidence Sir Hugh had been known to fix the accused with a monocled eye and to say, 'You don't want to ask him any questions, do you? Good! Three months!' With the advent of C. U. Rudkin, J.P., all that gradually changed. The magistrates retired more and more frequently to consider their joint verdicts, and after the evidence had been heard; but Charlie, being a sensible and tactful man, was content for the new procedures to evolve gradually. In this way he avoided any open breach with the Baronet, who even came to like him—'Deuced clever—but not a bad chap.' With the Clerk it was different. Uncle Charlie disagreed with his legal rulings only when his conscience absolutely demanded it, but that was too often for Mr Ponsonby. He complained to the Chairman, who took Charlie aside after a long argument over the refinements of the law of constructive possession, and said, 'Rudkin, my dear fellow, we all know Ponsonby's a bit of an ass. But we mustn't make it too obvious too often, must we? Distant cousin of me wife's, don't you know.'

Charlie did know, but persisted in correcting Ponsonby's law, partly because he couldn't bear his own learning to lie unused, and partly because enmity between them was unavoidable. Charlie had become legal adviser to the village of Hedingham, and had stolen a significant part of Ponsonby's practice. No solicitor could forgive another lawyer for doing that, let alone a layman. Uncle Charlie drew wills, contracts and tenancy agreements. He advised on tenant right, the Married Women's Property Acts, manorial rights, immemorial rights, divorce, ancient lights, and the Game Laws. He acted as executor for numerous estates, and arbitrated in disputes. Consequently he was a sharp pain in the sides of the local attorneys. They hovered over him like hawks, watching for one injudicious break from cover; but my Uncle Charlie knew to an inch how far he could go in defiance of the Solicitors' Acts without being in danger of prosecution for breach of their monopoly. If Charlie had been only a poor man's lawyer, the neighbouring solicitors would not have cared, but he had rich clients also, who went to him for the best advice in the locality, and paid for it.

One of them was the Bishop of Lincoln, who had a troublesome rector not far from Brigg. The Reverend Mr Forbes-Watson was so idle that he was conspicuous for neglecting his parish even amongst his fellow clergymen in north Lincolnshire. He was a bachelor and lived in one room of a huge rectory that was crumbling about his ears. When I say that he lived there, it is an exaggeration. Every Monday morning he caught the train for London to stay at his club, the Oxford and Cambridge in Pall Mall, until he returned to his parish on Saturday evening. What he did in London was, apparently, nothing. The Bishop had hired agents to watch him, hoping to discover mortal sin; but if Mr Forbes-Watson left his club it was only for brief shopping expeditions, or for little walks in St James's Park to feed the ducks. The truth was that he spent Monday to Saturday reading the newspapers and magazines, chatting with his cronies, and eating four good meals a day. At the week-ends he slept on a truckle bed in the rectory kitchen and rushed through his statutory services of Mattins and Evensong to a congregation of one widow and two spinsters, whom nothing could dislodge. Choir, bell-ringers, sides-men, servers and flower ladies had all long ago disappeared. He was happy for near-by parsons to collect the fees for the weddings, baptisms and funerals that were his perquisite. If any parishioner wished to take Holy Communion, there was a notice in the church porch saying that he could do so by appointment, but none applied. Mr Forbes-Watson knew his Canon Law, and never uttered one unnecessary Lord's Prayer, nor recited one superfluous Creed. He did precisely what was required to hold the Bishop and his learned Chancellor at bay, and he lived apparently secure in his temporalities until the Bishop, on the advice of his friend Sir Hugh, engaged Uncle Charlie to deal with him.

When Charlie had agreed his plan with the Bishop, he went to the village and found a labourer with a consumptive child. He asked him to go to the Rectory early every Monday morning before the parson caught the train to London, and request that he should visit and comfort his dying son.

'We don't want that bastard in the house,' said the labourer.

'Yes, you do,' said Charlie, 'for a guinea a time. And in any case, you won't get him.'

'Only the money?' asked the labourer.

'For sure,' replied Charlie.

He was right, and after a month he went to see Mr Forbes-Watson and presented him with the evidence of his callous neglect.

'Within the law,' said the parson.

'Perhaps so,' replied Charlie, 'but we're going to have a go at you, all the same, in the Consistory Court to deprive you of your living.'

'You'll fail.'

'Possibly,' admitted Charlie, 'but whom do you think we shall brief?'

'No concern of mine.'

'I think it is. Our man will be Ryder, Q.C.—the biggest chatterbox, I'm told, in your club.'

The subsequent negotiations were unfriendly, but in the

end Uncle Charlie was appointed sequestrator of the living. He received the annual stipend of six hundred pounds, hired a resident curate for two hundred pounds a year, and paid the balance, after costs, to the Rector in Pall Mall, where he lived for the rest of his life—but drinking club port instead of vintage.

Uncle Charlie discussed these cases with Henry and impressed one cardinal principle upon him. 'If you can only think of a difficult solution,' he said, 'you're wrong. The answer must be simple enough to reproach all who failed to see it, and so obvious that an Archimedes would leap out of his bath.' This precept was beautifully illustrated in the case of Dickie Ducker's cock, where the whole village had been unable to see the plain answer to their problem until Charlie provided it. Dickie Ducker was the Hedingham carrier, and he had a cockerel which, almost as soon as hatched, showed signs of the arrogance and ferocity which later made him notorious. He began by killing his nearby rivals but, having grown to his full strength, he became restless for further conquest and began, fight by fight, to extend his dominion throughout the village. Chickens scratched for their keep and ran free in the stack-yards, so as soon as the hen-houses were opened early in the morning, Ducker's cockerel had free access to every other group of poultry in the neighbourhood, and he made use of his opportunities. At first, in the savage flush of youth, he killed other cockerels out of hand, but with maturity and the assurance of success, he was content only to rule, and those who acknowledged his superiority might live.

Dickie Ducker took great pride in his bird's achievements, and the two of them rose together a little before dawn. While Dickie raked out the kitchen fire and made tea, he kept an eye on his rooster who stood, with head on one side, listening as the sun rose for a crow that could even remotely be construed as a challenge. If unable to detect any sign of rebellion, he crowed derisively and strolled back to his hens, scattering the stones in the yard with a few powerful thrusts of his long legs. But if another cock had, in an unguarded moment, insufficiently muted his morning call, then Ducker's bird, after sounding a terrible warning of his approach, straightway set off down the street and over the Green, with his master not far behind, in search of the offender. Having found the rebel he either fought him to the death, with Dickie watching from any convenient cover, or accepted his surrender by contemptuously scratching out a few of his feathers. Before long there was no other cock of any spirit left, and the village had had enough. However, the problem of removing the offender was sensitive. Shooting him or poisoning him or merely wringing his neck was, in a subtle sense, taboo. He killed in fair fight and he was a splendid, admirable bird, deserving a decent and fitting despatch. Furthermore Dickie Ducker, careful to retain his champion, always paid generous compensation for the death of his victims, although it was not easy to make him hear the complaint. He affected deafness, and cupped a hand to his ear, leaned forward, narrowed his eyes and only understood after several repetitions. Also, he drew the line at mere loss of plumage. To such paltry claims, he had an invariable and conclusive answer : 'They foind theer owen cloaths !' In all the circumstances it would have been as despicable to kill Ducker's cockerel in cold blood as to shoot a fox in view of the hunt.

It was inevitable that the village should bring the problem, in all its delicacy, to Charlie Rudkin. He said that he would 'see to it', and a few days later he drove off in his trap to Lincoln. He returned in the afternoon with a square wooden box and something very much alive inside it. That evening, after nightfall, the box was opened in the hen-house, and out stepped a tiny cockerel no bigger than a pullet. His eye in the lantern light was an incandescent bead, his head erect, his neck proud and arched and vibrant like sprung steel. For the size of his body, his legs were long and thick with powerful thighs, and from his heels sprouted two murderous prongs, as sharp as needles. In short, he was a gamebird, bred for the cockpit, with untold generations of death behind him.

The next morning, Ducker's cockerel stood listening, as usual, in his yard for sounds of rebellion, and there came shrilling to his grateful ear a new trumpet note, high-pitched and unrestrained. He threw back his head and returned the call. Back came the echo, and the challenge was tossed from throat to throat until the village rang with the sound of impending battle. Then the contestants advanced through the streets, each pausing now and then to call the other to his doom. They met on the Green and faced each other, heads down, tails up, and feathers ruffled. Ducker's bird saw death before him, but never hesitated and rushed in first to the attack. However, for all his advantages of height and strength, he could only match the other in courage. After a mercifully short flurry of feathers the gamester had done his work. He mounted the body of the fallen champion and crowed a strange shrill call of triumph. Uncle Charlie caught him, in leather gloves, and put him in the box. Dickie Ducker picked up the corpse of his own bird by the legs and, with the body trailing behind him, he came over to pay his respects to the caged victor. 'Aye,' he said ruefully, ''ee's got a bit of foight in' im !' The Green cleared of spectators, the game-cock went back to Lincoln, and Dickie's bird provided his own funeral feast.

I have lingered over that story for the pleasure of repeating the name of Dickie Ducker, which seems to me to be the most euphonious I have ever heard. So I will indulge myself further by telling one of my grandmother's tales about Dickie's father, another Dickie Ducker who was also the Hedingham carrier. He used to take his dinner with him in the horse-van to eat it as he drove on his rounds of the villages, or into Lincoln. One hot summer's day his wife had provided him with an eel pie, and when he had taken a bite of this delicacy he realized that the contents were not as wholesome as they might have been. So Dickie Ducker incontinently tossed the offending pie over his shoulder and it went straight down the open shirt-neck of a tramp who was enjoying an unauthorized ride on the tailboard. My grandmother told me Hedingham tales of that kind as I lay in her bed as a child in the morning after grandfather had got up, and they so convulsed her with mirth that she could hardly finish them for laughter. Another which particularly appealed to her sense of the ridiculous was of Bobby Atkinson. He was a fussy, bumptious old fellow, and a great bore at village concerts because he always insisted on singing a song called, 'The Woodpecker Taps on the Old Oak Tree'. As Bobby and his wife were asleep in the dead of night, there came a great knocking on their front door. It had to be very loud and prolonged to rouse the Atkinsons, for they were heavy sleepers, but eventually Bobby unwillingly got up and went to see who it was. His caller was Butcher Billy, the village idiot, who said, 'Please, sir, I thought you'd like to know—there's someone on the Green calling you "tapper".' Bobby could have dispensed with this reference to his singing at that time of night, so he dismissed his visitor pretty quickly and returned to bed. No sooner was he soundly asleep than there was another fusillade on the door. He went down again to find that Billy was back to tell him, 'Mester! He's at it again!'

After those two irrelevant stories I must return to Charlie Rudkin. He had become a lawyer in all but qualification, a scholar in all but formal education, and the wise man of the village. Henry could not have had a better tutor. If the Rector had undertaken his education, he would have become learned in Latin and Greek, and little else. Under Uncle Charlie he was not only plunged into the intellectual issues of the day, but he was taught to use his mind to practical ends. Above all his feet were kept in the Lincolnshire soil. The original bargain had been that Henry should spend his mornings working in the market garden, and Uncle Charlie kept him to it: 'You're so full of the old Adam, my boy, that you can stick to his occupation.' If Henry ever protested that he could be better employed than working under the hare-lipped Sidney, who was a disagreeable taskmaster, his uncle would have none of it: 'There's nothing better for keeping the brain cool than hoeing turnips.' It was as well that the daily spell of market gardening kept Henry's brain at a moderate temperature, because his heart was soon to be inflamed again by a most unexpected development. He was invited to the Rectory for dinner and chamber music with the parson, the schoolmaster and, incredibly, Miss Nancy Pitt-Melville of Hedingham Hall. It had become known that she played the viola, but Henry had never dared to hope that he might ever play with her. Yet it was to happen.

The composition of the dinner party involved so conspicuous a social *mésalliance* that it could only have been achieved by music, the great disrespecter of persons. The sad fact of rural life for both the Reverend Mr Smith and Miss Pitt-Melville was that, if they wished to immerse themselves in the string quartets of Haydn, Mozart and Beethoven, they needed a cellist and another violinist who played well enough to make the intonation bearable. And nowhere within a ten-mile radius of Hedingham could they find such a cellist and violinist except in Mr Palfreyman and Henry Fisher. The dilemma for Nancy's parents was acute. The gentility of the Pitt-Melvilles was not very secure. They were now invited to the Stuff Ball but they could not yet be described as 'county' in the exacting Lincolnshire sense of the word as understood by Pelhams, Amcotts, Fanes, Chaplins, D'Eyncourts, Willoughbys, Custs, Heneages, Massingberds, Langtons and Nevilles. They still had a long way to go, and it didn't help that Nancy was most unaccountably and distressingly fond of music. Not as a young lady ought to be—content to tinkle Clementi on the Broadwood grand, or to accompany herself in a few decorous songs—but passionately addicted to the gruff deep-throated viola for which there were no nice pieces to play to one's guests after dinner, and which demanded that she should consort with others if the instrument was to be played at all.

Oddly enough, Nancy herself had a voice like a viola, and it was all the more remarkable for being quite inconsistent with her appearance. She was now fairly tall and thin. Her pale hair was still straight. Her face had lengthened and the slightly protruding teeth had not retracted. Nancy looked a typical witless female product of an English country house, and one expected to issue from her mouth a quick, high-pitched, nervous, upper-class yapping. Instead there came a slow deliberate deep contralto that caressed her words and enveloped them in a warm liquid sensuous resonance that was not only very beautiful, but sexually exciting to a degree that unfortunate men like the Rector found almost intolerable. Indeed, whenever Nancy dined with him, he found her voice so disturbing that for fear of committing some indiscretion he was obliged to divert his thoughts to the young parlour maid waiting at table, who would be in his arms before midnight. Yet Nancy's love of the viola was not to be attributed to a fondness for the sound of her own voice. It was the result of an accident. When she was ten her parents took her at Christmas to Lincoln Cathedral to hear the *Messiah* and, arriving late to a crowded performance, they had to accept overflow seats close to the orchestra and on that side of it where the bows of some of the violas were almost digging them in the ribs. That was Nancy's first experience of orchestral polyphony at close quarters and in the contrapuntal choruses she watched the violas waiting to pounce suddenly upon the theme. When they came in beneath the violins she was astonished that anything in the world could be so beautiful. The revelation continued with mounting delight to its culmination in the 'Amen Chorus' where the violas maintained their husky and singularly distinct part in that extraordinary convolution of sound.

That evening gave Nancy an imprinted love of the viola that no persuasion of her parents could erase. So in the end they accepted the inevitable, bought her a three-quarter instrument, and the Pitt-Melville cockaded coachman took Nancy and her ever-attendant governess weekly to Brigg for lessons with a very old and respectable lady called Miss Pemberton. By the time she was sixteen, Nancy was ready to play with others and insistent that she should be allowed to do so, but there was no one of her own social class in the neighbourhood, apart from the parson, for her to play with. On the other hand, there was no need to look outside Hedingham to form a string quartet if Nancy could be allowed to play with a schoolmaster reputed to have left London in disgrace, and with the son of a blacksmith only recently turned tenant-farmer. Eventually, after long and anxious discussions with the Rector, whose impeccable background must have blinded Nancy's parents to his present domestic practices, it was conceded that she might dine monthly under the eye of her governess at the Rectory, and then play nothing more romantic than early Beethoven in consort with an old Etonian and two members of the lower middle classes, all of whom were immensely better educated than she, and rather better players.

The dinner-parties that followed were a torture to the parson on account of Nancy's voice, a delight to Henry, and of little importance one way or the other to Mr Palfreyman, who was unsociable by temperament and careless of high living. Mr Smith kept Nancy as far away from him as pos-. sible for fear that conversation with her might lead to an involuntary laying on of hands, so Miss Martin sat on his right at a circular table with Henry next to her, then Nancy, then the schoolmaster and so back to their host. Since the Rector was subdued by his inner conflicts and the schoolmaster was naturally taciturn, the welcome burden of making conversation to entertain the ladies fell upon Henry. He could do that without difficulty. My mother told me that her brother could never come home after a day's work without having done something amusing. She said that whenever he entered a room the atmosphere lightened because he came in smiling, bursting with something to tell, and full of charming confidence that everyone was delighted to see him. It was this remarkable *brio* that made him so attractive to women, for he was certainly not good-looking. Apart from his extremely fine and delicate hands there was nothing in his appearance that anyone would notice. Yet he held Nancy and her governess entranced at the Rector's dinner-table from the first mouthful of soup to the last walnut. Lincolnshire accent and all, they had never before heard anything like it. He talked with the whole of his body, shifting about in his seat as he switched his attention from one woman to the other, arms waving, eyes flashing, and now and then rocking back and forth in his chair with laughter. He did imitations, mimes and parodies, and occasionally rose from his seat to act little scenes. It was all very ill-bred, but highly entertaining. He ate cheerfully with the wrong knives and forks, tucked his napkin under his chin, wiped his bread in the gravy, and accepted second helpings with alacrity.

He had learned how to behave by the time I first remember him at family parties, but he could still hold even his own relatives fascinated by his conversation, notwithstanding that his brothers and sisters were well used to him, many were themselves compulsive talkers, and all loved the limelight. I can well understand the force of his youthful impact on Nancy Pitt-Melville. He appeared at once so vulgar and so brilliant, relaying Voltaire's jests in dreadful French, making fun of Nietzsche, and telling malicious stories about the Duchess of St Albans with as little respect as about his father's cowman. Yet when another guest picked up the conversation, Henry had the natural grace not only to give way, but to listen intently as if he would be delighted to do nothing else for the remainder of the evening. Although his table manners were deplorable and his accent was as broad as Lincoln High Street, he did otherwise manage by the untutored light of nature to be the almost perfect dinner-party guest—as ready to be entertained himself as to entertain others, no matter how hard the going might be. And the going was not very easy. The different social backgrounds of the Rector and his guests made common subjects of conversation difficult to find and demanded nicely calculated distinctions in modes of address. The Squire's daughter, for example, was 'Nancy' to the parson as a young equal, and to the governess as her pupil; but the schoolmaster called her 'Miss Pitt-Melville', and so did Henry—'Nancy' would have been too bold and 'Miss

Nancy' too servile. The parson addressed the schoolmaster with a lordly 'Palfreyman'. The governess, to assert the dignity of their common calling, conceded 'Mr Palfreyman' and Nancy did the same because she was young. Henry fared the worst of all, being 'Fisher' to everyone. After having had his dignity affronted at the first dinner by Nancy addressing him as if he were her coachman, Henry went home and asked his Uncle Charlie why Nancy and he, being of the same age, should not address each other on equal terms. His uncle hit that nail very firmly on the head : 'Because her father owns fifteen hundred acres, and your father is tenant of a hundred.'

After dinner the party retired to the Rector's large, bare, oak-panelled music-room, where four pedestal music stands in mahogany, each with a pair of lighted candles in silver sconces, were set out in a square. The instruments were removed from their cases and the players sat down waiting for the Rector to strike a tuning fork on his knee and then to hold it on the bridge of his fiddle so that all could hear the resonance. Four A strings were adjusted to the same pitch, followed by more shifting of pegs till the other strings were settled into their acrid fifths. That done, Nancy and the schoolmaster checked the unanimity of their C strings. Then the parts were put out on the stands and the players were ready once more to attempt the impossible—to play four stringed instruments in tune with each other. The problems of intonation are never completely solved by the best professional string quartets, if only because in the natural scale of voice and strings the sharpness of F in the key of G, for example, is a matter of opinion. Consequently amateur string quartets, at their most accomplished, are characterized by a sound that is restless, edgy, querulous and unfulfilled, even when it is not absolutely unpleasant. 'Why do they do it?' the organist of Lincoln Cathedral once asked in bewilderment when he happened in Minster Yard to overhear four middle-aged ladies maltreating Opus 18, No. 4. If he had been a string player he would have known that men and women become addicted to that strange torture of the musical senses because, within a string quartet, they can feel more intimately inside the mind of a composer than in any other medium. However, what appealed most to Henry about playing Haydn, Mozart and Beethoven at the Rectory was not so much the opportunity it presented to appreciate the distinction of those gentlemen's minds: it was rather the facility it provided to delight in the beauty of Nancy Pitt-Melville's eyes. Orchestral players must watch their conductor, but chamber musicians must watch each other. They sit facing inwards in a hollow square for that very purpose and the vigilant governess was bound to find no impropriety in Nancy and Henry from time to time exchanging glances over the top of their music. Moreover she would have needed a miniature score, and the competence to read it, before she could judge whether they did it more often than the music demanded.

Henry found string quartets an incomparably better cloak for dalliance than the church choir. With a lift of his bow in Nancy's direction before it descended on the strings, and with a passionate look into her eyes, it was to Nancy as if he were toasting her beauty and to her governess as if he were moved by the music. The Rector, of course, understood him perfectly, and the schoolmaster thought his playing affected. After a few months, Nancy smiled less when their glances met, and her eyes began to be troubled by her own response to the entreaty of his. Though she could not yet be certain that Henry was making love to her, she found herself glancing at him to see whether he was, and in this way complicity was established. Nancy found her situation difficult. Pride demanded that she should put an end to the impertinent advances of a blacksmith's son, but what could she do? If she complained it was open to Henry to plead innocence and ridicule her conceit. She could imagine the stories he would tell in the village of her supposing him to be in love with her. The obvious solution was to withdraw from the quartet, but that would be to give up her greatest pleasure on the mere suspicion that Henry was treating her with disrespect. In any case, it was only her pride that sought an end to his attentions. As a young woman she responded to them, and before long her grey eyes began to hold Henry's blue ones in an anxious blend of resentment and affection. He was now ready to use his knowledge of the grounds of the Hall, where he had trespassed as a boy. One night after quartets he engaged Nancy in polite and impersonal conversation as she was putting her viola away in its case and allowed her, but no one else, to see that he had slipped a note into it. The paper read : 'Every evening next week at six o'clock I shall wait for you under the old beech in the south-east corner of your park. If you do not appear at all I shall be distraught, and if you appear with your governess I shall be disgusted. Henry Fisher.'

On Monday, Tuesday, Wednesday and Thursday Nancy checked with a pair of binoculars from her bedroom window that Henry was as good as his word, and on Friday she ordered a groom to saddle her horse and rode off punctually to the beech tree to meet him. To have delayed till Saturday would have been too obvious.

'Well, Fisher,' she said, without dismounting, 'what is the meaning of this?'

'I had hoped that we might . . .' Henry paused, as if prepared to accept suggestions, but Nancy was unhelpful.

'That we might what?'

'Be friends?' he asked, with a smile that confessed a want of entire candour.

'I have enough friends, Fisher,' she replied, leaning forward to pat her horse's neck, as if to identify one of them. 'And if we are to continue, as I hope, to play music together, it would be as well for us to remain acquaintances.'

'You can say that easily enough from up there,' said Henry. 'But could you come down off your high horse and then dismiss me so contemptuously?'

'Most certainly!' she replied, dismounting and standing directly in front of him. 'And now, Fisher, will you kindly go!'

'And could you,' Henry persisted, 'kiss me and then send me away?'

Nancy hesitated, and then laughed. 'Oh yes, easily! You conceited fellow! I can dismiss you after a kiss.' She held out her arms, with the horse's reins over one of them, and they kissed gently and deliciously, in spite of the teeth, till she slipped from his embrace.

'Henry,' she said, in her deep voice, 'it's impossible. I'm not another village girl to roll with you in the hay like Lucy Lancaster. So please go. And don't bother me again!'

Lucy Lancaster was a surprise. He had no idea that Nancy was so well-informed, but he took encouragement from her jealousy, and noticed that she had not remounted. Instead, she stood stroking her horse's nose and looking miserable.

'Nancy . . .' he ventured, but before he could continue, she was in his arms again, saying over his shoulder, 'I hate you. I hate Lucy Lancaster. She's so pretty and so common. She's just right for you. And you're all wrong for me. Oh! Why did you come here?'

The upshot was that Henry took the reins of the horse and led it deeper into the shrubbery that surrounded the Pitt-Melvilles' park. Nancy followed and after Henry had tied the reins to a tree, they fell again to kisses and to youthful talk of loving each other. They agreed to make the shrubbery their meeting place, and that they should see each other no more than once a week for fear of discovery.

So when it was fine they lay side by side upon decaying leaves amongst the laurels and rhododendrons, and when it was raining they stood dripping in each other's arms beneath the pendant branches of a chestnut. They kissed interminably, drew the tips of fingers over noses and cheeks and explored teeth which sometimes snapped in play and bit. They ran hands through hair and nibbled the lobes of ears. They were bitten by ants and stung by insects, and were always uncomfortable. They whispered endearments and sighed and believed their love to be unique, while doing nothing that was not common to humanity. Henry swore that when he was rich he would return from Lincoln and claim her, and Nancy counter-swore that no other suitor

155

should approach her. They imagined that they were more happy and more sad than they would ever be again. The situation was, in truth, more exquisitely romantic than either would again enjoy; so romantic indeed that passion would have been an intrusion, an eager tongue or exploring hand a blasphemy. Infatuation at that level could not last, and it did not. Henry was seen going weekly in the direction of the Hall, and the news was passed from the village to Mrs Pitt-Melville by her lady's maid. The addition of the village gossip, the Rector's string quartets, and Nancy's new fondness for being alone in the park left her mother with a horrifying total. She challenged Nancy immediately, and the girl was too fine a character to deny her love. She was defiant, and even the threat to involve her father in this vulgar disappointment of all his hopes failed to extract a promise that her demeaning conduct would end.

Therefore Nancy's year at a finishing school in London was expedited. Within two days she was living with an aunt in Sloane Street to await the beginning of term. She wrote to Henry as soon as she arrived and collected his letters poste restante from a general post office. Ink and paper, however, were cold comfort. Henry soon afterwards went to Lincoln and Nancy did the Season. Within a year they were exchanging Christmas greetings, and within two years they were exchanging nothing. Henry never met Nancy again until several years after they were both married, and that is another story of a different kind. When my grandfather heard of the meetings in the shrubbery he jumped naturally to the wrong conclusions. 'Why, my boy,' he said, congratulating his son with a slap on the back, 'it must have been, with that poor thin creature, like shaking a bag of bones!' Henry did not disabuse him, but felt sick with disgust that anyone could fail to understand anything so beautiful.

Lucy Lancaster, who had been the thorn in Nancy Pitt-Melville's side, represented a change in Henry's sexual attitudes. After undergoing with Mrs William Anderson a baptism by total immersion in a sensuality that required nothing for its enjoyment but a mind closed to all else, he had hungered for erotic pleasures with a more cerebral content, though a discreditable one—the delight, for example, of disclosing Rebecca's breasts and gazing upon them in the confident knowledge that he was the first to do so with concupiscence. He longed to have the spoiling of a young thing, and sought rather desperately to seduce several virtuous little girls. If he had his will with any other than Rebecca, I never heard of it. Fortunately, the scope for satisfying tastes of that kind in Hedingham was limited, and he soon came to regard the pursuit of innocence as a tiresome and unrewarding endeavour. Even his success with Rebecca had proved a lamentable failure. So with that stage in his development behind him, he had been ready for Lucy Lancaster who was neither innocent nor virtuous. She was the nineteen-year-old daughter of a widow who kept the

Hedingham Post Office. Lucy helped in the shop and took her duties very seriously—selling stamps, taking in parcels, issuing postal orders, and keeping Her Majesty's accounts in a clear neat hand. In the shop she looked exactly as a diligent and conscientious assistant postmistress should. She wore a prim white blouse with narrow sleeves to the wrist, and fitting high in the neck in the form of a ruff. A long wide black skirt totally obscured her beautiful legs. On her fine straight nose she wore a pair of pince-nez glasses secured by a thin gold chain to her blouse. I have a photograph of Lucy in the post office manner. With the severe clothes, pedantic spectacles, her lips drawn tight, and a disapproving look into the camera as if it had under-stamped a registered letter, Lucy might, thirty years older, have been an early Principal of Girton. Yet this girl had men swarming about her like wasps around a ripe plum.

Lucy was slim-waisted, but gently rounded where advantageous. Her crisp brown hair was parted in the middle and flowed easily and gracefully over a pair of delicate ears to the back of her head. Outside post office hours, the pince-nez disappeared and the warmth of Lucy's brown eyes was revealed. The tight lips relaxed into gaiety, and the entire Lucy slipped into wantonness, as if her slow consumption and approaching death had lent pleasure a desperate urgency and made faithfulness to her betrothed a bitter irrelevance. He was an engineer called Jack Rushford, and by him Lucy had a little bastard boy, sired before he went to work abroad. Jack was due soon to return to England for the wedding that would legitimize the child and enable Lucy to die respectable. In the meantime she made love—not with all comers, but with a generous selection from a wide candidature. Henry was one of the elect, and Nancy Pitt-Melville had good reason to be jealous. Not only had he continued to enjoy Mrs William's favours while ingratiating himself into Rebecca's heart, but he could not forego the delights of loving Lucy while making eyes at the Squire's daughter over the music stands. Even during the meetings in the shrubbery, although terrified that his perfidy might be discovered, he had been unable to renounce his share in Lucy's generosity. However, not long after Nancy's departure to London, the consumption rapidly grew worse, and my grandfather began to take Lucy for drives in his trap so that she could have an abundance of fresh air. He was almost certainly one of her lovers. Then, a few weeks later, Lucy was suddenly taken to bed with another baby. Grandfather asked her why she had told no one, not even her mother, that she was pregnant. She replied simply that she had expected to be dead before the child was born. 'No,' said my grandfather, 'with consumption nature ensures that you live long enough to have the baby.' Henry and he were only two of the many suspected of being the father. It was an open question, but the man most widely held to be responsible was Charlie Berryman, the Duke of St Albans' gamekeeper. When his noble employer heard of it, he taxed him with paternity and, being puritanical, threatened him with dismissal. Berryman denied it, but the Duke was not satisfied. He consulted the Rector of Hedingham, in whose pastoral care the mother was, and told him of his intention to dismiss the offender. 'What?' said the Rector. 'Dismiss him because they say he's the father? Why, they say I'm the father too. And if Your Grace hasn't been mentioned, then you're the only man in the locality who hasn't!' It was an exaggeration, but it served its purpose.

Lucy gave birth to a healthy girl and Jack Rushford returned shortly afterwards to find his fiancée dying. To save him the further mortification of discovering a child who could not be his, the baby was kept hidden by Lucy's mother during Jack's visits to Hedingham, and they were married by the Rector in Lucy's bedroom as she lay coughing and the bridegroom stood beside her. A churlish priest would not have done it, but Charles Smith was kind and deeply understanding of human frailty. He stumbled a little when the Prayer Book required him to say that marriage was ordained for the procreation of children, knowing of the two conceived without the Church's blessing and that the bridegroom was ignorant of one of them; but he could tell

Lucy easily enough that it was also ordained for those who do not have the gift of continency. The service reduced him to tears with its reference to 'so long as ye both shall live', and to Jack and Lucy continuing together 'in holy love until your lives' end'. In fact, Lucy bore the ceremony with greater fortitude than the parson because she had more than the marriage service to remind her that she was dying. The wedding over, she sank into death through the heat of an intolerably hot summer in her little stuffy room. My grandmother used to send soup over for her and slices of chicken. The calling of the cuckoo that July was incessant. 'Oh! If only they could stop that cuckoo!' cried Lucy, but in vain. However, she managed to die before her husband knew of the second child and could reproach her for it. At the same time her sister Harriet, aged fifteen, lay in a shelter in the garden, in the grip of a galloping consumption. The Rector buried Harriet only a month after her charming, pathetic, naughty sister, whose funeral cortège had included her husband, my grandfather, my Uncle Henry, the gamekeeper, and many other men who came openly to weep for her.

Henry had celebrated his seventeenth birthday a few months before Lucy's death. It was time for him to leave Hedingham and go to Lincoln. By now he had no doubt what he wanted to do there. He would become a lawyer like his Uncle Charlie, but a qualified one. The only question was how. One branch of the profession was totally closed to him because the Benchers of an Inn of Court would never have allowed Henry to eat their dinners, and no barrister, however indigent, would have taken him as a pupil. The Bar was largely a preserve of the upper classes. Even solicitors, the lesser breed within the law, had their principles and tried to exclude boys like Henry from the profession. Entry was by way of a five-year unpaid apprenticeship, and the usual premium for articles of clerkship was two hundred pounds. The State also played its part in discouraging the poor from becoming lawyers. The stamp duty on articles of clerkship to a solicitor was eighty pounds, many times the annual wage of a farm labourer. So even if Henry could have found a solicitor willing to take him, he had no money to pay for his articles, and no means of keeping himself alive while serving them. Thus his ambition to become a qualified attorney could only be realized if someone in the family would provide the money. His father had none, but there were two possibilities—Aunt Kate and Uncle Charlie. Neither was helpful. Aunt Kate had left home penniless and had made money unaided. She was intolerant of silver spoons. She would help my grandfather and others struggling on the road to success with loans but, like a banker, she expected an untried beginner to earn, save, and risk his own money before he risked hers. 'I don't bet on horses,' she said, 'but if I did, they'd be over half the jumps before I'd stake a farthing.'

Uncle Charlie was unwilling to find the money for other reasons. His daughter Louisa was now fourteen and her devotion to Henry had only increased since he went to live under the same roof. It would have been unreasonable to expect him to remain chaste until Louisa was of marriageable age, but it was one thing for Charlie to be reasonable and another to see his daughter's floods of tears as the news broke of one amour after another. Henry had tried to keep the jealous daughter and doting father ignorant of his adventures, but village gossip invariably kept them well-informed. Also, though Henry simulated affection, he was not battling with indifference—it was a positive dislike, shared by the whole family. No one, except her father, could bear Louisa. Even Auntie Rudkin found her a trial. She was pert, opinionated and intolerably spoilt. Money was lavished upon her to an extent that was thought shocking and unprincipled. In all else Uncle Charlie was a modest spender. While rich by Hedingham standards, he continued to live in what was no better than a cottage. He ate well, but his table was not extravagant. His clothes were unassuming. Although a Justice of the Peace and a County Councillor, he did not edge himself towards the gentry by keeping a hunter, or buying himself into a shoot or a trout stream, as the newly prosperous are inclined to do. The family would have thought that vulgar enough, but it was even worse to prink out his daughter in silk dresses, to have her mincing through the village in patent leather shoes when everyone else wore boots, and to bedizen her petticoats and knickers with lace. 'That child,' said my grandfather, 'looks as if she'd been spawned by some smart dentist in Gainsborough!' The Fishers were scandalized to find Louisa doing the rounds of her cousins on the first girl's bicycle to be seen in Hedingham, not only gleaming with stainless steel, green enamel and 'Singer' in gold letters, but equipped with a wicker basket for her belongings and two paraffin lamps. The village school, of course, had not been good enough for Louisa Rudkin. She went instead to Robert Anderson's house to share the governess with his daughters until Charlie committed the ultimate inanity of sending her to boarding-school. Only my grandmother could find anything good to say about that: 'At least the little madam, with her gold necklaces, will be out of sight for nine months of the year. I shall be able to visit Auntie Rudkin without being sick.' Everyone thought Charlie demented, and Matilda was particularly shocked at his want of *savoir-faire*. Only the middle classes sent their daughters to boarding schools. The gentry had governesses. Louisa would acquire the most dreadful affectations: 'I suppose she'll come back sticking her little finger out when drinking tea, like Mrs Threlfall, the vet's wife. Or she may even hold her knife like a pencil!'

Therefore it is understandable that Henry could not take to his cousin Louisa. She was pretty enough, with large brown eyes and glossy well-brushed hair. As the maid Sarah Bell said, 'Night and morning, I've worn down the bristles of four brushes on that swollen head!' Louisa had no charm and far too much self-confidence. Even at the age of fourteen she was revealing the readiness to form opinions, and to express them, that was ultimately to make her the first woman mayor of a populous borough. So Uncle Charlie needed no great insight to realize that if his daughter was to have what she most desired—her cousin Henry—it would not be for love, but for money. Consequently he determined that his nephew should wait for financial help until Louisa was old enough to marry him, and only have it then on terms. Nevertheless, his son-in-law elect ought now to be set on a road that could lead, after the nuptials, to legal qualification. So the first step was to get Henry's feet under the table in some legal practice in Lincoln. The articled clerkship could come later when Louisa was Mrs Henry Fisher and money became plentiful. This scheme was not put forward in those terms. Uncle Charlie spoke of the need for Henry to have four or five years' experience in a legal office to be certain that he liked the law before committing himself to articles. Louisa, though not actually privy to the plan, could see and approve its drift. 'Just think, cousin! What a terrible waste it would be for father to spend all that money before you were quite *sure* !' An adoring look into his eyes, and the pressure of a childish hand, told Henry all too clearly what he had to be sure about. He cursed Louisa silently, and recalled the words of Aunt Kate when she had refused him a loan: 'If you can't start any-where and finish where you want to be, then you're no good!' Therefore he would go to Lincoln and be an office boy, but never, never marry Louisa Rudkin. And somehow he would become a solicitor, if only to spite her.

Bearing in mind the contingency that Henry might, as Louisa's husband, require articles of clerkship, Uncle Charlie had to find a solicitor in Lincoln who would be willing, if the need arose, to promote him from office junior to potential lawyer. That was not easy. All the respectable solicitors recruited articled clerks from the more solid public schools. They mistrusted brains, and measured character by skill with balls of different shapes and with oars. Win-chester bred boys who were clever enough to falsify the client account, and Eton bred them with tastes expensive enough to make it imperative. So provincial solicitors favoured the three R's—Rugby, Repton and Radley. The products of other institutions of a like kind they could accept, but not a boy whose only physical skill was in market gardening and whose education had been unreliable to the point of absurdity. Charlie did not waste his time on the legal establishment. Instead he went to see his friend Reuben Symons, a clever and cultivated Jew, who had insinuated himself into legal practice in Lincoln by putting up a brass plate outside a two-roomed office in Silver Street, instead of buying a share in an existing firm. Reuben was therefore a pariah, and his practice was of the lowest type. He litigated for workmen against their masters, for unmarried mothers against their seducers, for disappointed legatees against executors and for deserted wives against their husbands. He was an underdog lawyer but not, I fear, from principle. It was by necessity, because the comfortable and prosperous passed his door and went to the well-established practices on the reasonable assumption that their money and their confidences would be safer. Nevertheless, Reuben's practice was growing because he tended to win his cases. He had moved into larger premises, and he had a vacancy for a boy if he was bright, hard working, and reasonably honest. The prospect that Henry might in a few years' time wish to enrich Reuben by two hundred pounds in return for articles did not dismay him. Henry was taken to Lincolr for interview and Reuben accepted him as an office junior and potential articled clerk, at a wage of eight shillings a week. Whether Henry liked his new master was not very material, but in fact he did. Reuben was small and fat, with sharp little eyes behind gold-rimmed glasses. He had the broad hooked nose of his race, and his speech retained a Jewish difficulty with some of the interdentals and fricatures. He was restless, as if unsettled by an overactive intelligence, and though obviously good-natured, he gave the impression that he would stick at very little: 'In zis office, my boy, ve must take two tricks viz every trump. Ve don't have many.'

The next problem was to find Henry somewhere to lodge. The trouble that my grandmother took to arrange accommodation for a youth of seventeen able to look after himself seems a strange and uncharacteristic excess of maternal solicitude. The explanation is that the Fishers did not travel. They could not afford it. My grandfather only left England once, when Uncle Petro came over from Greece and took him on a short visit to Scotland. He was then well over fifty, and at dawn from the night train on the edge of the Northumberland cliffs he watched the sun rise over the German Ocean. For an experienced traveller dawn from the railway near Berwick is breathtaking. For my grandfather it was overwhelming because it was his first sight of the sea. Yet for forty years he had lived within twenty miles of the Lincolnshire coast. When Henry went to be interviewed by Reuben Symons, he saw Lincoln for the first time in his life. Until then he had never been further from home than Brigg and Gainsborough : he had lived for seventeen years within a radius of twelve miles. And the Fishers were in no way exceptional. Only a few people travelled, and they were usually the more prosperous. Even tramps spent their lives shuttling between the same two or three workhouses, a few miles apart.

Grandmother had no experience of her family going off here and there to stay in hotels, boarding-houses, or whatever other lodgings they could find. They left home very seldom and only then to stay with relatives. If a married uncle or a maiden aunt had lived in Lincoln there would have been no problem—Henry would have lodged within the family—but there was not even a third cousin. So unless a friend could be found to have him, Henry would have to lie within the gates of a stranger. Grandmother did not coddle her children, nor fuss over their welfare. Plain food and hard living was all they ever had, but they lived in a clean, ordered, well-regulated household. My grandmother was appalled at the thought of her son living in a slipshod environment, eating overcooked vegetables and retching at the sight of a rancid frying pan. Lodging-houses had a reputation that corresponded with her worst fears. Above all, his landlady might not sufficiently air the beds. Grandmother had a fearful dread of damp ones. She may have had no medical grounds for her apprehension, but it must be remembered that the mattresses were filled with feathers.

Only those who have slept on a huge rectangular cushion stuffed with down into which the body sinks within its own deep mould, like a precious instrument in soft velvet, can conceive the horror of being engulfed in a wet one. Through the long nights, moisture would seep into every joint of the body. It would penetrate the chest wall and ooze into the lungs. My grandmother earnestly believed that everyone crippled with rheumatism had at some time slept in a damp bed, and that every consumptive could attribute his end to that beginning. Aunt Pat's gnarled hands and twisted limbs were a legacy, not only of the laundry, but of London land-ladies careless of the need to keep an empty bed primed weekly with hot-water bottles or heated bricks to drive out the invading moisture. Therefore it was imperative for Henry to live in Lincoln with someone who could be trusted at least to keep his feathers dry and his blankets aired. In the absence of a relative it must be a friend, and fortunately Polly Baxter, whom my grandmother had known when she was in service in Lincoln, was still living there.

Grandmother wrote to her, and Polly replied that she had a spare bedroom and would be pleased for the son of her old friend to come and live with her. The following Friday grandfather was persuaded to get out the trap and take grandmother and Henry into Lincoln. Since it was market day, he could spend his time inspecting the live-stock while the other two went to see Polly Baxter's estab-lishment. To go out in the trap with grandfather was always an adventure. If he said he was leaving at eight, the wag-goner had the horse harnessed and the conveyance in the yard by seven fifty-five. Grandfather then climbed into the driving seat, the brake was off, the reins were in one hand, and his pocket watch was in the other. At one minute before the appointed hour, he shouted, 'Missis! It's eight o'clock. I'm off!' Grandmother was at this moment still in her bed-room adjusting the ribbons of her bonnet, and she knew that if she didn't fly down the stairs and into the trap within the minute, she would arrive in the yard to see it disappear-ing down the drive. Several times he had agreed to take her to Brigg market and had left alone because she was a few seconds late. However, it must be said that he never left early. He may have been an unpleasant husband, but he was a fair one. The next hazard was the journey itself because he was marvellously mean over his horses and thought he was shrewd enough to outwit a gipsy. Confident that he could get the better of them, he would buy the most unreliable creature from Romanies if it was cheap enough, because he prided himself on being able to control anything. In fact he drove badly, with a slack rein, smoking his pipe, staring at other people's crops and criticizing them. Frequently one of his vicious bargains would overturn the trap, so his wife and children were always fearful of riding with him. But in an emergency he kept his head, as on the occasion when he managed to get my grandmother upset out of the trap, and wedged in the shafts between the horse's crupper and the footboard. Lodged there she was conveniently placed for an assault by the horse's heels, yet he somehow managed to pacify it and to pull out his wife unkicked to death. Another acquisition was Old Jess, who turned out to be a jibber : if she took it into her head to stop, nothing would move her. They put ropes round her neck and pulled as if in a tug of war, but it was no good. Until she chose to move, she stayed. Old Jess was 'light-legged'— half trap-horse and half cart-horse, so she could in theory be used for both purposes, and that had been her attraction. But she objected strongly to ploughing, and jibbed incessantly when put to it. She took more kindly to the trap, but even so she would often and most inconveniently jib on the road into Brigg or Gainsborough. Yet another good buy was grandfather's big black gelding called Clumpus. The name was a corruption of Columbus, and the horse had acquired it by proving himself a great explorer, with an aversion for the beaten track. It was almost impossible to keep him on the highway in the country. Even the streets of a town could scarcely confine him, and one market day in Brigg he took my grandfather through a shop window.

However, the chestnut gelding that grandfather put into

the trap that Friday to go to Lincoln was, of all his horse-coping bargains, the most docile and clean-looking beast. Billy had been at the Glebe for several months and had given no trouble. All the way to Lincoln he went splendidly and they were within a few hundred yards of their destination, the Great Northern Livery Stables, before anything untoward happened. Then, as grandfather drove under the Stonebow, the horse pricked up his ears and increased his pace as if he knew that the stables awaited him only a little farther down the street. He took them over High Bridge at an eager trot, but made straight for the tram terminus at St Benedict's Church where, in the middle of the road, he aligned himself accurately between the lines and made off, without a glance at the stables, straight down the track towards the other terminus at Bracebridge. Nothing grandfather could do would bring him to a halt until they reached St Mark's Station where there was an official tram-stopping place. There in response to his driver's impatient tuggings and curses he stopped, willing for a passenger to alight. By now grandfather realized where the gypsies who sold Billy so cheaply had obtained him. After years of experience in front of a horse-tram up and down Lincoln High Street he had been superannuated by the Tramways Company. So grandfather had to dismount and lead the horse by the head back to the Great Northern stables where, with the greatest reluctance, he was persuaded into a stall.

Polly Baxter lived in Bailgate, and grandfather could have dropped his passengers there on his way to the Cattle Market, but grandmother wanted to start downhill in Lincoln so that she could take Henry to see Dr Hewson's house where she had worked as a young girl. She had few opportunities to relive her Lincoln past, and did not intend to waste this one. She had left Redbourne in 1865 at the age of sixteen to work for the doctor, whom her father knew well. Otherwise he would not have let her go. James Hewson had started life in 1798 as a baker's son, but a doctor was so impressed by him that he encouraged him to attend night school. Then his patron paid for him to go to medical school, where he qualified with distinction, being a very able young man. When my grandmother went to work for him in 1865 he was very prosperous, living in a large house in Newland on the west side of the city. He had spent forty thousand pounds, it was said, in acquiring a library which he kept in an oak-panelled room called 'the museum' with access from his conservatory. All this Henry heard, and a great deal more, as they stood outside the house and peered on tiptoe over the wall into the garden.

Grandmother's job was to look after this sixty-seven-year-old man as if she were his valet. He had already suffered one stroke, but his routine was to rise at four in the morning for a bath and a cold shower. For the sake of decency he had a lad, rather than my grandmother, to bathe him. Then, in dressing-gown and slippers, he ate egg and bacon for breakfast and at five o'clock he went to a nearby barber's shop to be shaved. On his return, he was partially clothed by the boy, ready for Bessie to take over to adjust his white shirt, frilled and gophered, and to tie his cravat. Then she fixed a white silk handkerchief round his neck, tied at the back in a little knot, so that she could brush his hair and eyebrows. If she knocked him carelessly with the brush he used to say, 'Never mind, bairn.' At six o'clock his coachman brought his gig and he would drive perhaps twenty miles away to Ancaster to see a patient.

In the evening Bessie had to read to him for hours, or brush his hair or rub his feet. As he sat he would strain towards the window and say, 'Who's that passing in the street?'—as if she, a stranger, could possibly know. She loved the old doctor like a father, even though he always opened her letters and then apologized for it, saying they were all right. He treated her like a child because he had lost his own legitimate ones. His wife had borne eight children who, without exception, died in the womb or very shortly after birth. My grandmother attributed this to tight lacing. One daughter lived for six months before dying in convulsions. Dr Hewson photographed her in her last hours so that he could have a large oil portrait of her after her death. This vigorous old man still maintained what my grandmother called a 'kept woman' in Lincoln who had five children, but not all were his. In the end she was his undoing because he fell one night when leaving her and only lived a month afterwards. After the fall his mind was affected and he was unable to recognize anyone. He left his lady-love an annuity of only one pound a week in recognition of the children who were not his; but all her brood were left a great deal more irrespective of origin, because he wasn't sure of the paternity of any of them and wanted to be certain of not depriving his own. Mrs Hewson was given six hundred pounds a year, which was a small provision in relation to his total wealth, and the substantial residue of his estate went to a pretty young niece who had recently caught his fancy. Grandmother stayed with the widow for a few months while the large house was sold and Mrs Hewson found accommodation more commensurate with her annuity. Then in 1867 Bessie went to work for Miss Snow at Atherstone Place in Eastgate.

This was the next stage in the sentimental journey. From Newland grandmother and Henry walked up the Steep Hill, past the Castle and into Eastgate. There he learned that Atherstone Place and Atherstone Court were two parts of what had once been a very big house belonging to the Suttons, one of the undoubted county families of Lincolnshire. When grandmother had arrived at Atherstone Place as Miss Snow's housemaid, the adjoining Court was the home of a widow, Mrs Brooks. The servants at the Place included a man called Chambers, a cook called Maria Blow, and six other retainers who ministered to the needs of the lady of the house and her feeble-minded relative Mr Chris. One of them was Polly Baxter, and that is how grandmother met her. Polly had been courted for seven years by Harry Hickinbotham, a joiner. They had bought a house, the wedding presents had arrived, and the next day they were to be married. Then, the night before the nuptials, Harry visited Atherstone Place and had cause to go to the closet where he suddenly expired. Whatever poor Polly's reactions were, Maria Blow was sufficiently moved by emotion to fall into the wildest hysterics, which she did at every possible opportunity. Another arose when the Prince of Wales, later Edward VII, visited Burgursch Chantry in St James's Street, which was Squire Chaplin's Lincoln house. Apart from a retinue of nobles and gentry, there was an army of valets, ladies' maids and other servants who were housed in Atherstone Court by arrangement with Mrs Brooks. There they organized a dance for the servants, and my grandmother and Maria Blow were invited. In the course of the festivities and under the influence of the liberal refreshments, Maria Blow at first started to giggle and then to weep. She ended in a fit of hysterics and lay kicking about on the floor. Bessie asked for the usual remedy—ammonia. But they brought ordinary household liquid ammonia by mistake and some was spilled on to Maria's lips. This brought her to her senses but made her very ill, and she accused Bessie of trying to poison her so that she could have Maria's fiancé, another Harry. Grandmother's reply was characteristically to the point: 'I could have your Harry without poisoning you!' Earlier in the party, she was smuggled over by Squire Chaplin's servants to Burgursch Chantry to have a peep at the Prince, who was about eight years older than she, as he crossed the hall on his way to dinner. While he was dining, she slipped into the cloakroom and tried on his hat, but at that very moment the Prince came in to relieve himself, and saw her wearing it. She hastily put it back on the peg and ran out of the room, though not before His Royal Highness had managed to pinch her disappearing behind.

Miss Snow was related by marriage to the Town Clerk of Lincoln, and his brother Mr Chris, who was weak in the head, lived with her under the care of his attendant Chambers. I have a photograph of Chambers and Mr Chris standing side by side like Tweedledum and Tweedledee. They are equally tall, though Mr Chris is the more portly. Each has his black frockcoat unbuttoned from the neck downwards to reveal identical waistcoats and narrow trousers in pale grey. Both wear very high black top hats, wider at the crown than at the brim but at their narrowest about half-way up, like the cooling towers of a power station. The two men stand arm-in-arm, but whereas Mr Chris rests his free hand upon a furled umbrella, Chambers has thrust his into a pocket at the back of his trousers. A little dark spaniel sits impartially between them, and nothing distinguishes master and servant except the superior smile of the attendant and the vacant stare of the attended. It was one of Chambers's duties to walk Mr Chris round and round the circular lawn at the front of the house, like a bear on a chain. Mr Chris had an allowance, but he was never allowed to spend it and this deprivation made him so angry that he would throw his useless sovereigns into the fire until the attendant eventually persuaded him to make salvage easier by drowning them instead. The servants brought Mr Chris a bucket of water, and the drowned coins were then carried out to be dried and distributed in the kitchen. It was, of course at Atherstone Place that my grandmother had met Miss Snow's nephew, the first Edward Fisher; but loyalty to his successor forbade her to tell Henry anything about it. So she walked on in silence towards Polly's shop in Bailgate, thinking sadly of her lost love.

Before I describe what Polly Baxter had to show my grand-mother by way of accommodation for Henry, I must explain how she advanced her fortunes from being a housemaid in Atherstone Place to owning the freehold of a shop in Bail-gate. It came about on the excellent advice of the attendant Chambers after the untimely death of Harry Hickinbotham. If Harry could have delayed his seizure in the closet by twenty-four hours he would have left Polly his widow of an afternoon instead of his disappointed fiancée of seven years. She would then have inherited on his intestacy the house she had helped to buy and furnish. As it was, Polly was entitled to nothing. Everything went to Harry's parents, who did not like her because she had supplanted in Harry's affections the girl they had hoped he would marry. Consequently his father and mother kept all, and Polly lost her seven years' savings as a housemaid, amounting to twenty pounds. When Chambers heard of Polly's further disaster, he advised her to retrieve her lost fortunes by becoming the housekeeper to an old man. Moreover, he could find her the very situation. His Uncle Albert, the retired chief clerk to a Lincoln corn-merchant, had recently lost his wife and needed someone to look after him. Uncle Albert was believed to have some money laid by. 'It's up to you, Polly,' said Chambers, 'how you persuade him to leave you enough to buy a little shop when he's gone. But there are ways. What do you think?' Polly thought it was a better idea than staying with Miss Snow in the hope of another suitor appearing, so she went to keep house for Uncle Albert in Monks Road. Mr Chambers was seventy-two, with a good crop of white hair and mutton-chop sidewhiskers. He was small, rubicund and usually cheerful, though when Polly joined him he was still cast down by the loss of his wife, to whom he had been devoted. A large studio photograph of the departed Rachael hung over the chimney-piece in his living-room. She wore a white mob cap and a voluminous black dress, and her eyes stared at Polly over her long nose as if she had a shrewd idea of what the housekeeper was up to.

Polly did not want to be again forestalled by a premature demise, so she went quickly to work to secure her position. She cooked her master delicious little meals, kept a bright fire blazing in the living-room hearth, took him for walks in the fields around Greetwell for the good of his health, and saw to it that he had a pint of strong Newark ale every evening to restore his spirits. When she brushed the dandruff off his coat collar she stood rather closer than was strictly required, and sometimes as she put down a plate of nourishing stew before him at table, a loose strand of golden hair might touch momentarily in passing a white whisker. After supper he sat on one side of the fire reading the paper, and Polly sat sewing on the other, while her master from time to time stole surreptitious glances round the edge of the *Chronicle* at an ankle disclosed a little too freely by the negligent crossing of his housekeeper's legs. Every detail of Polly's campaign was carefully contrived. All the personal ironing was done on the living-room table in his presence after her intimate garments had blown immodestly in the wind beside his on a clothes-line at the back of the house. The ironing done, she folded his coarse woollen underwear with the reverence due to some rich chasuble and piled it upon her own linen, catching his eye to see if he had observed the juxtaposition, and he always had. If Polly retired early to bed, she did not fail to come down again to give Mr Chambers his bedtime cocoa, and her dressing-gown was never clutched so tightly to the throat as to hide completely the lace-covered outline of a well-formed bosom.

My grandmother had a photograph of Polly taken when she was at Atherstone Place. Her face was too long and her eyes were not deeply enough set for her to be beautiful, but she had a good figure. At the age of twenty-six, she was handsome enough to drag the thoughts of an old widower away from the past and into the present. One of the few consolations for a man in growing old is that the range of his appreciation of women widens with every decade. Those who would not have stirred him when he was twenty become, by a merciful provision of nature, objects of desire in his declining years when, unless he is rich, he cannot reasonably expect any longer to enjoy the beautiful. Therefore it was not long before Polly's gentle assault upon the old man's senses had its intended consequences. One evening when she came down in her night-clothes to give him his cocoa, Rachael's picture had been turned to the wall. Before she could ask why, the widower's lips were upon hers and a mottled hand was exploring the lace top of her nightdress. They then took themselves to bed, where Polly found that Mr Chambers was entirely capable, although he made love as if against his will, with deep sighs of regret—almost angrily. Polly nevertheless enjoyed the triumph of her charms over his conscience and met his brusque and resentful caresses with bites and scratches, because she had reservations too. After all, she was only in his bed from necessity. So their mating was fierce, cat-like and erotic. It was also very satisfactory. With Mr Chambers, Polly reached fulfilment, as she never had with Harry. This surprised her, but need not have done. If old men can make love at all, they can usually do it well, because age has dulled the sharp edge of sexuality. Years later Polly told my Uncle Henry: 'You boys! You're like rockets—up, bang, a shower of sparks, and it's all over. My dear old Albert could hardly get off the ground, but when he did, he went on almost for ever.' The 'Albert' was a familiarity Polly allowed herself after he was in the grave. Between the sheets, he remained 'Mr Chambers'. Neither of them ever referred to their love-making, as if it were something better not mentioned. Life in Monks Road continued as before, except that when twice a week the picture had its face to the wall, Polly knew that she was expected across the landing. Conversely, when once a month she turned it outwards again, Mr Chambers knew that his housekeeper was not available.

The old clerk had told his dying wife that he would not remarry, and he never did; but after a year of unlawful matrimony, Polly told him of the wickedness of Harry's parents, and received a promise that if she stayed with him till his death, he would see her provided. Five years later he died suddenly and quietly in the night. Polly arranged his obsequies and then, not having heard from his lawyers, she went to see them on the excuse of wanting to know what was to be done with the house. Mr Chambers had employed the corn-merchant's solicitors, one of the better firms in Lincoln, because he had transacted, as chief clerk, much of his master's business with them. After a long wait in a dingy passage, Polly was shown into a room with one high dusty window. The walls were covered by dark mahogany cabinets and piles of black japanned deed boxes with white lettering on the sides—'Monson Estates'; 'Abraham's Charity Trustees'; 'Witham Commissioners of Drainage'; 'The Honourable Charles Heneage'; 'Dean and Chapter', and other such indications of the respectability of the practice. In the middle of the bare wooden floor was a large desk that had once been flat-topped, but was now piled high with yellowing bundles of paper, each tied with red tape nearly brown with age. Polly was asked to be seated on what was no better than a kitchen chair, and she saw over the top of the papers the upper half of the face of Mr Rogers. He was the senior managing clerk, well over eighty, and knowledgeable beyond belief in the affairs of many citizens of Lincoln in the distant past, but now tending to be forgetful of recent events. When Polly announced her business, he rubbed the back of his head and started to dig about amongst the bundles, like a hen scratching for corn in a stack-yard. 'Hmmmm ... Chambers deceased ... Monks Road was it? Hmmmm ... Did you say we'd got probate?' Polly knew neither what probate was nor whether they had it. Eventually Mr Rogers concluded that they probably hadn't, so he turned his attention to a huge black cast-iron chest, supposedly fire-resistant, in which he had for more than sixty years thrown every will he had drawn and seen duly executed. He struggled with the heavy lid until Polly went to help him. Then he searched in a disorganized way through the contents till Polly's sharper eyes saw the bundle 'A. Chambers Esquire', and picked it out for him. He pushed his steel-rimmed glasses up on to his forehead and held the packet almost against the end of his nose to identify it. 'Ah! There we are.' They sat down again, with Polly in a fever of impatience while he slowly perused the will, his lips moving silently as he read. When he had finished he pulled down his glasses again and peered across the haystack at Polly. 'I'm sorry, Mrs Chambers, but it seems that after a few inconsiderable legacies he left the whole of his estate to a person described as "my faithful servant Polly Baxter". Naturally, as his widow you can dispute the will—allege undue influence perhaps—but you'll have to go to another firm of solicitors. We couldn't act for you.' 'But I'm Polly Baxter!' she protested. Mr Rogers was unperturbed. 'Then in that case, let's hope we don't have too much trouble with the widow.' In the end all was made clear to him, and Polly left in the happy assurance that she was thenceforth richer to the extent of about three hundred pounds, after costs and expenses.

Polly sold the house in Monks Road and invested the proceeds, and most of her other spoils, in the freehold, stock and good will of a sweet and tobacco shop with living accommodation in Bailgate. The business was profitable enough to make Polly independent of the need to take a lodger, but she was prepared to have Henry to oblige a friend. The question was whether her establishment would satisfy my grandmother's requirements. The first impression was favourable. The outside of the shop gleamed with fresh paint, and the lettering 'P. Baxter—Confectioner and Tobacconist' on the fascia board was neatly executed and well spaced. As grandmother pushed open the door she met the resistance of a catch, and the sudden release as she over-came it set jangling a bell that hung from an arm of thin sprung steel screwed to the inside of the door. The pealing of the bell died away as the agitation of the spring subsided, but only to be renewed when grandmother released the door and a heavy lead weight on the end of a cord pulled it shut again. Polly had responded immediately to the initial sum-mons and she came into the shop by a door that led from her living-room. 'Bessie Millson! And after thirty years, not many months older!' That was more polite than truthful. Grandmother was over fifty and the effects of time and matrimony were noticeable. Polly was of the same age but, with the advantages of independence and several hundred pounds in two and a half per cent Consols, she had worn less. The long fair hair that Mr Chambers had loved to see unbraided and streaming over her bare shoulders and around her naked breasts was now grey and tightly bound in a bun at the back of her head. But whereas grandmother had grown thinner, Polly was heavier and the increase in tissue had cushioned her cheeks from sinking and her skin from falling into folds and creases. She was beyond the shoals of middle age: a secure, well-preserved, healthy spinster, no longer troubled that she would never again attract a handsome man. The horizon of her sensual pleasures was bounded by comfort, warmth, cream cakes, and a glass of brandy in the evening. It could be said that Polly Baxter knew no better than to be happy. If she read anything, it was the *Lincolnshire Chronicle*. George Eliot, Keats and Browning never enticed her into their anxious minds. The Cathedral Choir could wail the 'Agnus Dei' in

Byrd's Four-part Mass without piercing her sensibility with disquiet. Polly was easy, kind, contented and dull—an ideal landlady. Nor was her accommodation less suitable. The living-room was behind the shop with a kitchen beyond. There were three bedrooms, and Henry could have the one at the back to study in quiet. Grandmother's critical eye could hardly fault Polly's domestic regimen. The windows were clean, the lace curtains recently washed, each family photograph stood on its own circle of white lace, the antimacassars bore no trace of stain from a careless head, the oak and mahogany gleamed with beeswax and turpentine, and the brass coal-scuttle shone like a cavalry breastplate. The cakes and pastries she offered for their refreshment were airy and delicate. The bread and butter was paper-thin and the glass bowl of potted meat had its mantle of melted butter, a lace doily and a sprig of parsley. Grandmother could peer into the spout of Polly's teapot and see no stain from previous brown libations. But what she most approved was the bulge of a hot-water bottle under the blankets in the back room : it showed that Polly aired her empty beds. So the bargain was concluded. Henry would lodge in Bailgate with all found for four shillings a week. 'What do you like, love, for supper?' Polly asked. 'For myself, I'm partial to a trotter.' 'Well, Aunt Polly, it's like this,' Henry replied, feeling that with so many aunts already he might add another without straining the concept, 'What I really like to eat is anything. Indeed everything—if it's as delicious as your potted meat.' 'Ah ! He's a sharp one,' said Polly, 'flattering me already !' But she was pleased at being his adopted aunt, and at the prospect of feeding a hungry boy who carried about him a promise of the unexpected.

Grandfather had agreed to collect his wife and son from Polly Baxter's shop, and there was still an hour before he was due. Henry went to look at the Cathedral after an admonition to be back on time, or he would lodge with Aunt Polly sooner than had been arranged. Grandmother wanted to fill the precious remaining hour in Lincoln with a visit to

Newport Cemetery where, in his early grave, lay one of her past lovers. When Edward Fisher had been banished from Atherstone Place to Australia, she was courted by a young printer called Charles Favell. After her death we found three mementoes of him beneath the lining paper in the bottom of a drawer—a photograph, a Valentine and a poem he had composed complaining of rejection. Grandmother had been sufficiently moved by Charles Favell to retain a sentimental attachment to his memory, but not enough to marry him. His photograph is well preserved by years of darkness. It shows a handsome young man with fair hair and wide-spaced intelligent eyes. He is beautifully dressed with a white cravat, a fine barathea jacket with silk facings, and a double-breasted waistcoat of the same material with wide sweeping lapels like the jacket. His contrasting trousers have very narrow stripes and are cut close to his long legs. Even his pose is elegant and studied. He leans with an elbow resting on the head of an upholstered chaise-longue. His weight is on one leg, with the other lightly crossed over it. A curtain is draped in a curve behind him to balance the opposite inclination of his body. Perhaps Charles Favell was too elegant to appeal deeply to a robust woman. The Valentine is ornate even by Victorian standards. It has layers of thin paper superimposed upon each other in intricate patterns and fretted like lace, all to provide an oval frame for a poem headed 'True Affection' and full of banalities: 'fairer far . . . thy kindly heart . . . the winning grace . . . a guiding star . . . thy pure and generous mind'. Although Charles Favell was a printer, the poem in the Valentine is not his. The manuscript saved by my grandmother shows that he could write better than that. She had refused to marry him, so he chides her with dignity and, in the first four lines, with a fair talent:

Thou can'st not call me faithless,
For never vow of mine
Was breathed and lightly broken.
But was it so with thine?

Go mingle with the thoughtless
And revel with the gay;
Leave me the sad remembrance—
That dream of yesterday.
My last farewell is spoken,
One sad word lingers yet.
Although my voice may falter
My heart would say 'forget'.

Forget my grandmother never did. The eloquent printer died unmarried before he was forty and, while waiting for her husband, grandmother went to see her lover's grave. She visited it again when she was a widow of ninety. By then the cemetery was disused and Charles Favell's grave was overgrown and neglected. She traced with a trembling finger the lettering on his stone, worn to illegibility by storm and frost.

The journey back to Hedingham was uneventful enough for grandmother's thoughts to linger with the two men she had loved. Then, safely arrived at the Glebe, she went to bed with the man she had married. Henry walked from the farm to the cobbler's house and found Charlie Rudkin reading in the front parlour. His uncle put down the book and asked if his accommodation was arranged. 'To my mother's entire satisfaction,' said Henry. 'That's just as well,' said Charlie, 'because your service agreement with Reuben Symons isn't arranged to mine!' Reuben wanted to have Henry under covenant not to work for any other solicitor within a twelve-mile radius of Lincoln Castle for a period of ten years after leaving Reuben's employment. It was the usual device employed by solicitors to ensure that their clerks, however able, could not substantially better themselves. The reason for it was this. A solicitor's clerk might by experience and study become a good lawyer. He might also have a manner that inspired confidence. If so, he built up his own personal clientele of those who came for advice to him rather than to any of the partners by whom he was employed. Bills were delivered for the work he did as if it had been done by a qualified lawyer, but the clerk was paid a salary only. All the profits went to the partners. Even a fair-minded solicitor could not share them with his clerk because solicitors were forbidden by law from sharing their profits with anyone other than a solicitor. It was, of course, a law made by lawyers. Parliament was full of them. Barrister M.P.s scratched the backs of solicitor M.P.s, and the service was returned. Even so, the system would have been defeated if a clerk had been able to sell his services to other solicitors in the locality and to take his clients with him. Then he could have commanded a salary almost as high as the profits attributable to his clientele. Therefore every solicitor taking a clerk put him under covenant not to work for another solicitor in the district for a number of years sufficient to ensure that his clients would have forsaken him before he could attract them to a rival firm. Here another group of lawyers lent their aid—the judges. They enforced these covenants by injunction, notwithstanding that they were in restraint of trade and contrary to the Common Law. The covenants had to be limited in time and in area, but the judges held that it was reasonable for solicitors to stretch the time long enough, and to extend the area far enough, to ensure that a clerk was effectively prevented from changing his employer within his home district. Thus the judges connived at a solicitor's clerk becoming a kind of bond-slave. They justified it by saying that if the interests of the employer (always dear to the judiciary) were not thus protected, a solicitor could lose his clients by the defection of a clerk to a rival firm. This argument was specious. If the clients would leave with the clerk, it was demonstrated that they were his clients and not the master's.

Uncle Charlie's Liberal free-trading principles were outraged. Furthermore, being himself an unqualified lawyer and under the constant threat of prosecution for encroaching upon the privileges of the legal profession, he detested their restrictive practices. He had also his daughter to consider. When Henry married her and became a solicitor, Louisa would want to be able to hold up her head in Lincoln society. That she could never do if her husband stayed in Reuben's litigation practice. So Henry must eventually be bought a share in a respectable conveyancing and probate firm, but the covenant would prevent it because Reuben had left no cranny of the law unstopped. The restriction extended to Henry practising as a solicitor in Lincoln after qualification. 'The Common Law,' said Uncle Charlie, 'is supposed to be a bulwark against oppression. And so it is— except when lawyers are the oppressors. This covenant is a monstrous denial of liberty. Yet take it to Reuben's ermine-coated brethren in the High Court, and they'd sprinkle the foul thing with holy water!' Charlie threw the offending document back on to the table, and paced about the room, banging his clenched fists together in a fine show of Benthamite indignation. 'I won't have it! Rest assured, my boy— I won't have it!'

The date of Henry's departure was postponed. The following week, Uncle Charlie went to Lincoln to upbraid Reuben for daring to present such an unconscionable agreement for his approval. 'But, my dear Charles,' protested Reuben, 'he's a bright boy! If he comes to me and zen leaves vizout zis covenant, he'll take half my practice. Vell . . . perhaps not half. But too much!' Charlie banged the table. 'How many clients do I bring you when I can't deal with them myself because of your damned monopoly?' 'You bring me quite a lot,' conceded Reuben. 'Then take your choice! Either you lose my clients now, or my nephew's later. Which is it to be?' Reuben wriggled and twisted for half an hour to get off that hook, but in the end Uncle Charlie landed him. He had known before he put the question that his friend would settle for the present certainty and accept the future risk. 'Very vell, Charlie. Give me ze agreement. I'll cut out ze covenant. But I expect a lot of verk from you. You'll play fair viz me? Yes?' 'Of course,' said Charlie. 'You'll have the work—until my nephew's ready to handle it.' The value of the service Uncle Charlie rendered to Henry in preserving him from bondage was, as it turned out, immense. Several years later he was able to move to another practice on most advantageous terms.

When the agreement with Reuben was signed, sealed and delivered, grandmother insisted that Henry should return to the Glebe for his last few weeks in Hedingham. So the morning came for him to labour for the last time in Uncle Charlie's market garden under Sidney's unwelcome supervision. Cousin Louisa was home on holiday from the ridiculous boarding-school, and she hung about the greenhouse where he was pinching out the side shoots on the cucumbers and repotting fuschia cuttings. She was almost in tears at her cousin's imminent departure from under her father's roof, but she had retained sufficient presence of mind to make herself attractive. Henry had once praised the school uniform that suited her very well, so she was wearing it. A shallow cylindrical straw hat with a band of blue ribbon sat straight across her forehead, tipped forward in the upper-class manner. From beneath the brim, a pair of large brown eyes settled upon her cousin with reproach for leaving her. The grey woollen blazer with blue silk edgings hung open to show a gleaming white blouse and a gaily striped tie pushed forward by the sprouting of a very tolerable bosom. Louisa Rudkin at the age of nearly fifteen was precocious in more than conceit. She had already rounded into womanhood and this was also apparent in the way her pleated grey skirt fell over her hips. On this occasion she had dressed to please her cousin, but it was not unusual for her to bicycle about in Hedingham in uniform to demonstrate that she went to a school for young ladies. In that she took a pleasure that was innocent, but the practice also afforded opportunities for one that was not. It enabled her to go to her room to change at a time, just before dinner, when Henry also went upstairs after his morning's work in the garden. Even in a Victorian household, members of the family occasionally caught glimpses of each other more or less naked, because few remembered all the time to be on guard, and still fewer were devoid of curiosity. But the frequency with which Louisa forgot to close her bedroom door was unusual, and Henry seldom hurried past it. Cousin

Louisa might be vexatious, but no one could deny that she was pretty, with her long black hair, bright intelligent face and beautiful limbs. In various stages of undress she was well worth having a peep at as she moved about her room, or bent over the washstand brushing her teeth with Calvert's powder. Always too late she would acknowledge Henry's presence on the landing and run to close the door with little false cries of alarm. Louisa provoked her cousin because she loved him with a fierce passion that made her reckless of the consequences. Hitherto there had been none, because she was jealous and troublesome enough without encouragement. If Henry had so much as kissed her in earnest she would have become intolerable; but now he would soon be out of range of her affection, and he had an account to settle. She owed him an articled clerkship. To trifle with her and then depart would help to balance the books.

On this last day at the cobbler's house, Henry expected a final performance. As dinner time approached, Louisa sat on the greenhouse staging swinging her long legs, and staring sulkily at him as he worked in silence. He saw her depart for the house and after allowing her time to undress he followed. To tell Louisa of his approach he scraped his boots noisily on the iron ridge outside the back door. Then he slipped them off in the living-room, and went upstairs. As he expected, Louisa's door was ajar. She was in her petticoat, with one foot on a chair peeling off a grey silk stocking. The usual cry was raised, but it was Henry who closed the door—after he had entered the room. This was a development Louisa had not consciously intended, and she was about to give a genuine cry of dismay when Henry held his finger to his lips and smiled so reassuringly that she remained silent as he approached and took her into his arms. Then apprehension changed to excitement and her lips sought his without fear or reservation. He slipped an arm behind her knees and lifted her on to the bed. She lay there unresisting as, between long gentle caresses, off came the second stocking, the petticoat and a vest. By now Henry was demented by passion, and turned aside to undress. But when he bent once more over the naked girl intent upon folly, it was to find his cousin with one eye wide open, a shrewd look in it, and her legs firmly crossed. Louisa had recovered her good sense. Labourers' daughters won husbands by becoming pregnant. Ladies did not. Their husbands married virgins. That was the custom, and Henry would not seduce her today and marry her later. Therefore he must wait for the maidenhood, as he must wait for the articled clerkship. 'Oh, my darling!' she said. 'It will be so lovely when we're married!' Henry kissed her a perfunctory farewell. He ran a valedictory hand insolently over the body he hoped never to see again, pulled on his trousers, and went to his room.

Auntie had herself prepared a particularly good dinner to mark the end of Henry's four-year stay in her house. It was very kind of her because she was still not well, and the cooking was usually done by Sarah Bell. Whatever was wrong with Auntie's health had not improved. Nor, for that matter, had it become worse. Dr Rainbird now thought that her trouble was more likely to be asthma than consumption. She was not subject to violent or distressing attacks, but she was always short of breath. This made her speak in a whispering strangulated way, as if she couldn't raise enough air pressure to blow a good wind across her vocal chords. Air was for her a precious commodity. She put one foot before the other experimentally, testing whether she had enough oxygen in her lungs to complete the endeavour without provoking one of the attacks she so successfully avoided. Being what was called an 'invaleed' had become her role in life. Anyone new to the village asking who my grandmother was would be told, 'That's the wife of Mr Fisher at the Glebe.' The answer to the same question about Uncle Charlie's wife would be, 'That's Emily Rudkin. She's an invaleed.' This lent her a personal distinction separate from, and to some extent competitive with, that of her well known and dominant partner: whereas my grandmother, difficult though her marriage was, only occasionally resorted to illness as a weapon against her husband. She had once developed a serious attack of jaundice when he was being particularly objectionable. Otherwise she contented herself with fainting attacks, and calls for sal volatile, when one of the boys was about to be thrashed with unusual severity.

Although Auntie Rudkin made ill health her profession, she bore it with fortitude. It was bad form in my family to complain of illness. Auntie allowed her eyes to reveal astonishment at the rude health of others, but that was all. She did her best against infirmity and would trouble herself to make an occasion of Henry's last dinner. In the centre of the table was a bowl of walnuts from the old tree by the cobbler's shop, and a bunch of gleaming black grapes ripened in Uncle's hothouses and held back from the London market. The meal started with a large Yorkshire pudding in a round baking pan. It was cut in segments like a cake and eaten as a first course on its own, covered with thick brown gravy. Then the empty plate was returned to Uncle Charlie who carved the sirloin of beef, while Auntie served the roast potatoes, parsnips and Brussels sprouts. The last course was Henry's favourite pudding, a sherry trifle under a generous mantle of whipped cream decorated with blanched almonds and crystallized cherries. After dinner the retainers—Sarah Bell, Cobbler Jack and Sidney—were brought in and the whisky was brought out. Auntie Rudkin could accept a glass because it helped her breathing. Uncle Charlie would only drink wine. His unpleasant old father had in the end become so oppressed by the jeopardies of life that he had taken to brandy and died a drunkard. Charlie discovered in middle age that if he drank spirits of any kind he developed a marked inclination to do it frequently. Therefore, fearing a congenital weakness for the consolations of alcohol, he never now took any strong drink at all. Instead he kept a bottle of claret at hand, which he thought he disliked. Louisa was allowed damson wine, but she had no need of it to maintain her spirits. She was happily assured that Henry's approach to the threshold of delight had rendered him a lasting captive to her charms. Indeed, Louisa's cheerfulness at Henry's departure seemed perverse and inexplicable to all but Sarah Bell who had heard some bumping about and cries of pleasure in the bedroom as she laid the table for dinner in the living-room below. There were toasts to Henry's success in Lincoln, and much recalling of his early errors in horticulture. Of how, for example, he had pruned out the fruit buds on the apricots, and had earthed up the onions as if they had been leeks. They insisted on a farewell tune on his fiddle, and then he gave Auntie Rudkin a present for having been so kind to him. It was a case of stuffed birds he had bought at Brigg Fair for twelve shillings. Under a dome of thin glass, eight different little sub-tropical cock-birds perched incongruously together, each on its own fork of an upright branch. Amongst sprays of brown grasses, their wings were outstretched to show bands of red, green, yellow and blue. Gorgeous plumage clothed their bodies and mantled their heads with iridescence. 'Well,' said Sidney, 'wherever you caught them, it wasn't in these parts!' Finally, Auntie Rudkin thought it was time for her afternoon rest, so Uncle Charlie and Louisa took Henry and his box round to the Glebe in the trap.

When Henry returned to live temporarily at the Glebe before his departure to Lincoln, even grandfather did not ask him to work on the farm, so he enjoyed a few days of leisure and the first holiday in his life. But he was not idle. The front garden was grandmother's responsibility and it needed attention. Since any work for her was a labour of love, Henry spent his mornings in clipping, weeding, thinning, hoeing and raking. Enclosed by tall hedges, the garden stretched for about two hundred yards down to the village street. The lawn in front of the house was flanked by a pair of lofty yews, and by the hazel from which Cousin Charlotte had picked her two nuts for remembrance. There was also an old twisted walnut, and common lilacs, laburnums and philadelphus, grown with age and neglect into sprawling and interlacing trees. Beyond the lawn was a formal garden divided into squares and rectangles by low box hedges with gravel walks between them. Some of the enclosures were filled with old country roses, one with herbs for the kitchen, another with lavender that grandmother dried and put into muslin bags to lie in chest drawers to scent her sheets and

189

linen. Others had drifts of catmint on which the lithe farm-cats slept in the sun ; tall delphiniums, pale as if the rain had almost drenched the blue out of them ; clumps of blood-red peonies ; and spikes of the common iris, intense with pigment like a deep-dyed velvet. Rows of raspberries filled the next part of the garden, and large unpruned bushes of red currants, black currants and gooseberries. There were white currants too, now so little grown, but delicious when mixed with raspberries in a pie, or eaten in the heat of summer by a child wandering amongst the bushes and picking a laden stalk to be stripped of the fruit by drawing it between half-closed teeth. An orchard lay at the end of the garden by the village street, blowing in spring with the blossom of tall untended crabs, quinces, pears, plums, and apples in their varieties of pippin, codling, russet, pearmain and seedling. The entire garden had a charming air of neglect. Daisies sprouted in the lawns, and the dark green yew hedges grew at their own slow pace unchecked. The low box edgings of the gravel walks looked always in need of their next trimming, and the flower beds were never entirely clear of weeds. Grandmother's supply of child gardeners was restricted by the demands of the farm. She drafted them into her service whenever she could, but they were available too seldom for her gardening to be more than a rearguard action against the fecundity of nature. So grandmother had to be careful of her resources. The only bedding-out was in front of the house and the choice of plants, whether by indifference, economy or weariness of spirit, was invariable—geraniums, calceolarias and lobelia. Grandfather bought the plants in Brigg Market, his wife paid for them with the egg and butter money, and the children set them out and watered them from the pump. Henry was happy to render his mother a farewell service in a garden that was old and placid, with the trees and perennials exhausted by too many summers, and so unlike the parade ground on which he had drilled rebellious nature behind the bootmaker's shop.

The afternoons were spent in the best bedroom with his

190

brother John, who lay recovering from the rheumatic fever that had brought him back after he had run away from home. This was John's second attack. The first was undiagnosed and untreated in infancy, because no one knew of it until he began as a young boy to shake with St Vitus's dance, a disease of childhood due to injury to the nerves by rheumatism. The symptoms are spasmodic twitchings of the hands, knees and facial muscles, so the medical name for it is chorea from the Greek word for dancing. The popular name derives from the dancing pilgrimages that were made to the shrine of St Vitus. Grandfather was so affronted that a son of his should appear, by his unseemly jerkings, to be an idiot that he went to the expense of taking John to a specialist in Hull who said that he could cure the St Vitus's dance, but the remedy would leave the boy with a weak heart. 'Cure him,' said grandfather, 'and let him have the weak heart!' Therefore it was important that the second bout of rheumatic fever should do minimal further damage. Dr Rainbird came in his trap every few days to allow his leeches to graze on John's temples. The only other treatment was complete immobility. He was not allowed even to read, but had to lie motionless to avoid the least strain on his heart. So grandmother fed him with a spoon and he was hoisted with great care on and off the bed-pan. Although it was summer, the maid carried up coals in a bucket to keep a fire blazing in the cast-iron fireplace to avoid any risk of a chill. In the mornings old Thomas Millson sedated his sick grandson by reading chapter after chapter of *Edwin Drood*, *Barnaby Rudge* and *Bleak House*, which were his favourite novels but not John's. After dinner, when Thomas had retired for his afternoon rest, Henry came to talk about his life with Uncle Charlie, his loves and sensualities, and of what he hoped to do in Lincoln. The story of his recent adventure with Louisa included an account of her physical charms that made the patient's heart beat faster than was good for his state of health. John was astonished that dislike could have so obscured his vision. He had failed to notice that Louisa was becoming a beautiful woman, but now that he knew better he assured his brother, with the confidence of a handsome man, that her seduction would be his first convalescent activity. But Louisa was not to be won by regular features. She was a true daughter of her father, intelligent and complex. Only clever men could attract her, and her virginity was eventually cropped by an ugly youth called Cyril Jopling, the son of a Congregational Minister, and as persuasive a talker as his father.

John did not intend to stay for long in Hedingham after his recovery. He was nineteen before he first escaped from home, and James was eighteen. They did not leave earlier because if their father required them to work on his farm, they were under a filial duty to obey. All grandfather's sons, except Henry, laboured in his fields until early manhood. Now and again he gave them a few pence, and grandmother found them an occasional shilling from the egg and butter money. Their only other reward was accommodation, food and clothing. They had no thanks, and a great many hot-tempered cuffs about the head and kicks on the behind. John and James were grown men. They would have exchanged blow for blow with another male who struck them, but parental authority was such that their father could hit them with impunity. The only defence they had against their father's aggression was to put themselves out of range of it by leaving home.

John had reached that point one Saturday in June when Robert and he were hoeing mangolds in the Coldhams, and grandfather came to inspect the work. He said that some of the rows were badly done, and Robert pushed the blame on to John, alleging that the rows were his. John denied it, but his father came to strike him. Whereupon he dropped his hoe and ran out of the way. Grandfather did not pursue him, but went off saying, 'I'll get you when you come home to roost!' So John decided that his father should not get him. He walked, penniless, towards Brandy Wharf. One direction was as good as another so long as it was away from the Glebe. In Brandy Wharf, however, he met by chance Jack Harrison who knew the family and guessed that something was wrong. Jack was middle aged, rather deaf, entirely illiterate, rough and kind. He pretended to be in need of a lad to help with the smallholding on which he kept a few horses for towing barges on the Ancholme Canal that had been cut earlier in the century during the canal fever. It was still being dug in 1827 when the Duke of St Albans married widow Coutts, and the Irish navvies joined the wedding celebrations. The grounds of Redbourne Hall were thrown open for feasting. An ox was roasted whole upon a bonfire and the charred remains were distributed to the poor, of whom there were many. Barrels of beer were tapped under the trees of the park, and Irishmen poured into the grounds of the Hall like bears after honey. There they became so thoroughly drunk that a body of soldiers had to be called out to suppress the riot. It was not the only Irish offence. As the Duke and his lady were being driven through the village, one of the labourers waved the open carriage to a stop and held out a couple of pennies to the Duchess who, during her first marriage, had grown ugly and hirsute. 'Here you are, you old bugger,' he said, 'go and get yourself a shave!'

Jack Harrison persuaded John to stay with him, and sent his wife Ruby to the Glebe to tell his parents where he was. Grandmother was grateful to the Harrisons for befriending John, but it would not do for any offspring of hers to be working for a man who made a living by hiring horses to bargees, and was little better than one himself. It was still worse for John to be living in his house. She wrote to her Cousin Jenny Edwards in Gainsborough to ask if she could give John lodging and find him employment. Jenny's husband, who was a foreman in Marshall's engineering works, arranged a job for him there, and John moved to Gainsborough to live with Jenny and to work in Marshalls until he was sent home with rheumatic fever. This freemasonry of cousins, more or less remote, was invoked again by grandmother when James ran away shortly after John. In the light of his brother's experience, James went straight to Jack

Harrison for shelter and lived with him until grandmother heard of it. This time she asked grandfather's Cousin Miriam Plumtree in Nottingham for help, and she gave James lodging and found work for him on the railway. Miriam was the well-to-do widow of a pork butcher who had previously married her sister; but the first Mrs Plumtree died young and her consolate widower then made Miriam his second wife several years before Parliament granted the indulgence to marry one's deceased wife's sister. Fortunately the unlawful union was validated by the Act of 1907, but it never found favour with Miriam's Cousin Annie. Her response to the news of Mr Plumtree's second marriage was, 'Well! And I've been his convenience all my life!' Annie Fisher was also convenient to my grandfather. It was she who lent him fifty pounds to start farming, and was paid back in bed as well as in banknotes.

After John and James had left home Robert was only waiting for the day when he would be old enough to emigrate to New Zealand. He had recently left school at the age of thirteen, and was now working full-time on his father's farm instead of only the hours at either end of the school day. Although he was very tall, he was still young enough to suffer the cold formal thrashings that followed, a day afterwards, the commission of what grandfather, on a wide interpretation, regarded as an offence. For example, Robert was so short-sighted that he wore round steel-rimmed spectacles which he lost one day out in a field when stooking sheaves of barley. He was promised a thrashing if he couldn't find them, so he covered a large area on his hands and knees with his eyes six inches from the ground; but without success. After he had been given his thrashing and a new pair, he was able to go into the field again and find the lost spectacles almost immediately—only to have another beating for not looking carefully enough the first time. On another occasion, Robert came home cut and bruised. He admitted that he had been fighting and had lost. So grandfather gave him an immediate thrashing and told him that he would have another unless he went out and beat the vic-

194

tor, who was still loitering in the gateway to the farm. This time, of course, Robert was successful.

Of the other children, Matilda, George and Fanny were still at school. Mary was fifteen and lived at home waiting for someone to marry her. In a family where, as a matter of course, children were expected to work, Mary was the exception. Whereas grandfather required Matilda to milk the cows when she was old enough, and to feed the pigs, he never asked Mary to do anything. Her personality carried a negative charge powerful enough to generate lines of force around her that repelled work. Breaking through the field was so unpleasant an experience that few would undergo it, and even my grandfather was daunted. However, against her mother, whom she purported to love, Mary employed other tactics. Grandmother was neither foolish nor gullible but she was, like most of us, capable of being manipulated by trivial and superficial attentions. A husband, for instance, can more effectively charm his wife by scent on anniversaries and flowers on special occasions than by increasing her regular and unromantic allowance by many times the cost of the gifts. A prompt exclamation of delight at a new dress earns more matrimonial credit than a dozen hours at the kitchen sink. Mary was a master in this art of appearing to give all by way of devotion, while conceding nothing of any importance, and grandmother never failed to accept the shadow for the substance. Mary was the first to notice a change in the ribbons on her bonnet; Mary saw that her mother looked tired and brought a cup of tea, while chiding Matilda for her indifference; Mary knew when her mother had a letter for the post; Mary found her missing spectacles; Mary burdened herself with the prayer books as they walked to chapel, and guided grandmother needlessly into her pew. No one kissed her mother more effusively night and morning. Consequently, if the maid was busy and there were floors to scrub, coals to carry, water to pump, beds to change, slops to empty or fires to lay—Matilda or one of the boys was given the job. Mary's role was to make the cakes, to dust, to change the flowers, to do the delicate ironing, to sit about waiting to jump to her mother's light and personal service, and to remind her constantly of the laziness and inattention of others. In a simple world, Mary's face would have matched her character, but even Matilda, her major victim, had to concede that she was attractive. Thus nature, intent upon reproduction, baits her most barbed hooks. Mary had no shortage of admirers of her trim figure, fresh complexion, green eyes and brown hair in tight little curls. Conversely, she liked men and the pleasures they could provide. Alex Lancaster, Lucy's brother, was her current favourite, but not my grandfather's. It was enough that he worked in a grocer's shop in Kirton Lindsey and had a receding chin for him to be dismissed as 'a herring-chinned counter-jumper', unworthy even of Mary's hand. Nevertheless, she liked him and the family found him useful because he played the piano very fluently by ear.

Alex's services were in demand after nine o'clock in the evening when grandfather went down to the Royal George. The family watched the clock for him to leave the house— and he knew it. Then they could let themselves go and be as wild as a bear garden until the Royal George closed and all was quiet again. Grandfather went every evening, but he was not a heavy drinker. He never bought more than one pint of beer and he only drank whisky to seal a bargain made in the corn exchange or on the farm. Otherwise his sole indulgence, apart from women, was a mild addiction to his pipe. He went to the pub not so much to drink as to talk politics and to gossip with the Hedingham tenant-farmers and master craftsmen. Freehold farmers, like Robert Anderson, were too grand for public houses and kept aloof. Labourers and domestic servants were not welcomed. They could go to the Beauclerk Arms. Grandfather's pleasure in the company of his peers at the Royal George was to lay down the law on any subject that came up and to hear the local scandal. There were some good tales. Ted Atkinson, the wheelwright, had one of a young girl who was staying at a splendid Elizabethan hall near Lincoln, and was visited in her bedroom by a wicked lord, a fellow guest, intent upon spoiling her virtue. The poor girl escaped his clutches and ran out of the room in her nightgown. He pursued her along the landing and she fled up to the long gallery on the second floor. There she found that she was trapped. All the doors leading out of it were locked. As her ravisher approached, she opened a mullioned window and preferring, traditionally, death to dishonour, she threw herself out and landed on a large holly bush. It broke her fall and saved both life and virtue at one uncomfortable go. 'That girl,' the wheelwright said, 'was destined, one way or another, to be pricked.' All the men at the Royal George were given to bawdy anecdotes, and my grandfather was also given to boasting. Sometimes he paid for it. He talked of his brood of young turkeys roosting in the damson trees out of reach of the fox, and the next night they were all gone. He bought a mushroom brick and made a bed of manure in the dark carriage house. When the floor was covered in a fine crop of button mushrooms, he told his friends at the Royal George and by morning they had disappeared.

When grandfather took his departure for the pub, he was hurt that the children were unable to disguise their relief. Although he was harsh and unkind, he wanted to be loved ; but the joy of his absence was too keen to be hidden. My mother said of these hours, 'Happy childhood ! Friends in ! Wildest games ! Loudest music ! Riotous dancing !' They had the organ pianola, with its supply of slotted rolls, that relayed Sousa's marches, and the overtures to numerous operas. As one of the children pedalled away on the organ, Mary's lover hammered out an improvised accompaniment on the piano which had been tuned to the same pitch. Henry added variations and descants on his fiddle. Robert contributed on the mouth organ, the tin whistle or the Jew's harp. Grandmother could harmonize in a sweet alto voice below the treble of the young children. Sometimes they formed a little orchestra with combs and tissue paper ; and sometimes they cleared the table out of the way and danced. Always the living-room was full of noise and laughter, until grandfather came home again. Alex could only be there on Saturdays and Sundays because he had to walk over from Kirton. He was given a bed at the Glebe, supposedly in one of the boy's rooms, but in fact between the sheets with Mary who, of the three Fisher girls, was the naughty one.

During his brief holiday Henry immersed himself in nostalgic recollection of his past loves. Rebecca still haunted him and, on an impulse to scratch uselessly a sore place, he walked over to Snitterby to visit the Kirbys. Rebecca was now engaged to be married and no longer avoided him when he came to see her. She sat with the family and joined in the conversation. Studiously, every word, every inflexion, every gesture, conveyed that he had been an irrelevance, a nullity. In consequence, she was more attractive than ever and Henry learned that the discomfiture of initial rejection is as nothing to the ache of desiring a familiar body that has been withdrawn and made available to another. There was not much more consolation in visiting the beech tree in the south-east corner of the Pitt-Melvilles' park. Letters from Nancy had grown infrequent and were no longer ecstatic about the past. They were more concerned with her life in London. She was playing her viola in a chamber group, going to the theatre with her aunt, polishing her French, and already wondering whether the young subalterns of the Household Cavalry would prove during her season to be as stupid as she supposed. Nancy was cheerfully forgetting him. It was more satisfactory to linger by Lucy Lancaster's grave in Hedingham churchyard—so crowded by centuries of death that each new excavation by the sexton turned up teeth and bones of the previously departed. Lucy's father had broken at the Woodside Farm, leaving his widow too poor to buy her daughter a tombstone. She lay anonymously under a green mound that would sink as the ground settled. Lucy would decay, but never change. Henry's memories of her were preserved for ever from contamination by the present, and he was beginning to feel that she was the one he had most loved. So there was nothing for it but to take his violin again to the miller's house. Mrs William, however, was not prepared to forget that he had deserted her for the assistant postmistress. 'My dear boy,' she said, 'I will accompany you if you wish, but not to bed. I'm not a mattress for Lucy's ghost. Wait till you get to Lincoln. The wife of a minor canon would be more appropriate for spiritual gambols of that kind.'

Henry had other visits to make before he left. As Aunt Kate grew older she tended to spend more time at the Grange and she was in residence there with her friend Sally Overton. Sally was about thirty-five and good-looking in a severe way. Unlike Kate, who was ring-laden, heavily scented and thickly plastered with powder, Sally wore neither jewellery nor other embellishment. She was like a spare and dedicated suffragette. Perhaps Sally was more to Aunt Kate than a friend and business associate, but there was no overt speculation within the family about their relationship. There could be talk about the Rector's musical groom and his fondness for choirboys, but not about the possibility of erotic play between two women. It was too bizarre and outside rural experience. Whether Aunt Kate took Sally as her lover is uncertain. She might have done, because she did not like men and was bold and unconventional. Kate did not scruple to roll about naked in the mud in a paddock behind the Rectory in the belief that it was good for her rheumatism. She had just returned from one of these expeditions and was about to take a very necessary bath when Henry called at the Grange to bid her farewell. He was shown up to her bedroom, where Kate received him in a dressing-gown. The bath was in front of a blazing fire, and a maid stood by with great white enamel cans of hot water and a supply of warm towels. Kate found the mud in the Rector's field 'very beneficial' and was feeling invigorated and cheerful: 'Come round later for tea, my boy,' she said, 'and we'll have a talk. There are a few things I ought to tell you.'

When Henry returned to the Grange, tea was served by a parlourmaid in cap and apron. She brought in the silver tea service, the Royal Worcester china, and a plentiful

199

supply of tomato sandwiches and cakes. Kate, Sally Overton and Henry talked generally until Sally retired to her room and Kate became as generous with her advice as she had been careful with her money. This, according to my Uncle Henry, was the gist of what she had to say : 'I've no time, my boy, for the humble and meek. All that religious talk is for cripples of various kinds. Anyone sound in mind and body should at least try to be rich and powerful. I know of no pleasure keener than going to New York, Paris, Rome and London to see in the major capitals of the world my own name over my own property, and to have many nationalities working for me. Here at home I live waited upon hand and foot, surrounded by beautiful things brought from France, Italy and Greece, helping my family if I am so inclined, respected and sought-after beyond almost anyone, man or woman, in the locality. My boy, either you like that or you don't ! I do. And bear this in mind ! If you have the will to get on, there's nothing to stop you, because most people are incompetent. You'll meet a few who are too good for you, but never be afraid of the competition. So it's up to you. Come and see me again when you've shown you can swim without someone holding your chin up. Till then— goodbye ! I never wish anyone good luck. The right name for it is hard work.'

After that valediction, the next call was upon Mr Palfreyman who lived in a little house under the same roof as the school. Here Henry found, as later with the Rector, that the departure of a youth intending to make his fortune seemed to put an obligation upon the relatively unsuccessful to explain why they had not done better. The schoolmaster launched into an account of the career that had ended in a tiny house and a salary of eighty pounds a year. No scandal in London had driven him to Hedingham, as the village supposed : he had come for the simple reason that it was a great improvement on what he had known before. William Palfreyman had been reared in Stepney in a tenement near the London Docks where his father had picked up casual work on the ships. Some days they ate, and some days they did not, and William never wore shoes. His father died when he was eight, and thereafter his mother supported the family on poor relief and by taking in washing. She gave William the job of keeping an eye upon the ham bones in the butchers' shops. He had to be the only boy looking through the shop window at the very moment when the butcher cut for a customer the last slice of ham from the bone. Then William could go in and beg the bone for his mother. He was not the only boy in the district on a similar mission and each watched the others. When William estimated that a bone would be ready in a particular shop that day, he led his competitors for miles on false trails before he doubled back alone to secure the prize. No skeleton of a lost traveller was picked cleaner by vultures than those ham bones by the poor in Stepney, and then they were boiled for soup. But thanks to his mother, who was a fine resourceful woman, William was kept at school until, as the cleverest boy, he was invited to stay on as a pupil teacher. When the Hedingham post was advertised and William secured it, he came straight to the village from the slums of Stepney. 'My dear Fisher,' he said, 'when I was a boy, the height of my ambition was to eat regularly, to wear warm clothes, to be shod, and to have time for reading and music. And I've managed it. For me, that is success. Achievement depends on where you start.' Henry thought that it also depended on where you finish, but it was not for him to contradict one so recently his schoolmaster. So he thanked Mr Palfreyman warmly for his excellent education, and took his leave.

His farewells to the Reverend Mr Smith were made over dinner at the Rectory. There was no other guest, but the food and wines were as good as in the time of the quartets, the mahogany and silver were as highly polished, and the parlourmaid was as pretty. As she set out the nectarines, grapes and finger bowls, Mr Smith turned the conversation towards Henry's departure: 'So you're leaving us to seek your fortune! Well, well! It prompts me to speculate on what might have been my own career. I could today perhaps have been wearing gaiters and be entertaining you in a deanery; or perhaps a fractious don, and you my guest at a high table in Cambridge. In the event, however, we are dining in Hedingham Rectory—tolerably well, I hope, but in obscurity. It is, you will think, a sorry story.' He dismissed the parlourmaid, who departed with a demure curtsy. They then drank a great deal of port, and the Rector became more confiding. Henry heard in detail how Bridget Atkinson had drawn Charles Smith to Hedingham and how, in retrospect, he could see no feasible alternative to the course he had taken. The institution of matrimony bewildered him. 'Tell me, Fisher,' he asked, 'how do men of my age go to bed with the wives they married thirty or forty years earlier? Have those husbands some huge hunger beyond my comprehension?' Henry thought that unlikely, but remained silent. The Rector acknowledged that his love of women had condemned him to a country rectory, and to the atrophy of his intellectual talents. Perhaps he had chosen the wrong profession. In few others would mistresses have blocked his advancement. Even judges could enjoy the young and still reach the House of Lords. The Rector began to feel sorry for himself until he rang for the maid to refill the decanter. Discreetly he let fall the significant nod that summoned her to his bed that evening, and regained his spirits. 'Be that, Fisher, as it may! Here I am, and very agreeable it is— thanks to my private means and a good living. A little money helps to improve any situation, and I can only commend your determination to make some for yourself.' Henry thanked him for that benediction and rose to leave, but the parson stretched out a hand to stay his departure. He was disappointed that Henry had ceased to attend divine service. Perhaps the dogmas of the Christian faith were not, in the strictest sense, entirely true. If the Rector had been born a Turk, no doubt he would be a Mohammedan, but every society needed a humanizing and stabilizing influence, and in this country Christianity was the established religion, and the Church of England was the established church. The Anglican faith was the conscience of the upper classes amongst whom Henry, he supposed, hoped eventually to number. So he would be well advised to support it. Without the Church's humane and tolerant influence, English society would degenerate into callous opportunism or, by way of reaction, into an enervating and illiberal egalitarianism. My uncle had not expected to hear from one of its ministers so cool an assessment of the utility of the Christian faith, but he hid his surprise and assured the Rector that he would most certainly bear his words in mind. Then, after thanking him for his advice and the splendid dinner, Henry bade him goodbye and went home.

His farewells to the family were made at a special festivity one evening while grandfather was at the Royal George. The next morning the trap was at the door in good time and to the minute his father shook the reins and they moved off towards his new life with Reuben Symons and Polly Baxter. Thus, having set Henry on the road to Lincoln in the year 1899, I have now completed this account of his childhood and youth in Victorian Lincolnshire. In a few years the virtuous Queen will give place to her unvirtuous son, and that will mark the end of an era that I admire and see exemplified, without the hypocrisy, in my grandfather. Since I have told so many stories apparently against him, I will end as I began—with an acknowledgment of his worth. All his children testified to their happy, though often painful, childhood. His sons, as healthy males, left home as soon as they reasonably could, and all grew up sane and well balanced. So did his daughters. My grandfather's success as a parent was achieved in defiance of almost every rule the psychiatrists have taught us. But we are beginning to realize that they have a financial interest in being wrong: the more children they can disturb, the larger their adult clientele. As a husband, grandfather was not much more loved than as a parent, yet his wife was neither neurotic nor unhappy— partly because she was very busy, partly because she shared a common endeavour, and partly because her husband was worthy of respect. She could tell me many tales to his disadvantage, but none that reflected upon his honour. Grandfather was reliable and trusted in business. Throughout the neighbourhood he had a reputation for good sense and probity. He was firm, uncompromising, determined, and dedicated to his objectives. He had most of the qualities that make a civilization, and few of those that lose it. In a long agricultural depression he preserved a large family from poverty. His children had to work to survive, and they worked the harder for the beatings. In the end, grandfather owned his half a thousand acres, thanks to the single-minded courage, resource, tenacity and unconcern for others that, in a nation, builds an empire and earns the admiration of succeeding generations debilitated, under some inexorable law, by the success they can envy but not emulate. Grandfather was, in his small way, a great Victorian.

FISHERS

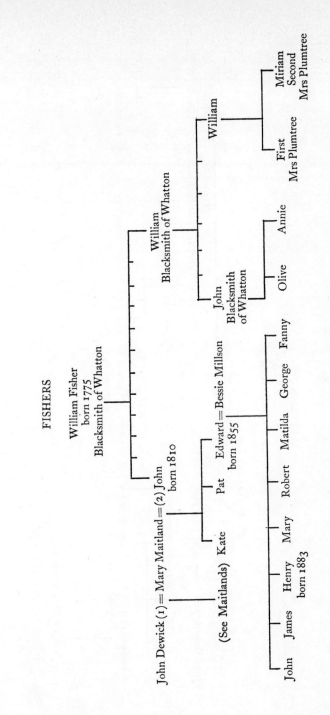

William Fisher
born 1775
Blacksmith of Whatton

John Dewick (1) = Mary Maitland = (2) John
born 1810

(See Maitlands) Kate   Pat   Edward = Bessie Millson
born 1855

William
Blacksmith of Whatton

William

John
Blacksmith
of Whatton

Olive   Annie

First
Mrs Plumtree

Miriam
Second
Mrs Plumtree

John   James   Henry   Mary   Robert   Matilda   George   Fanny
born 1883

MAITLANDS

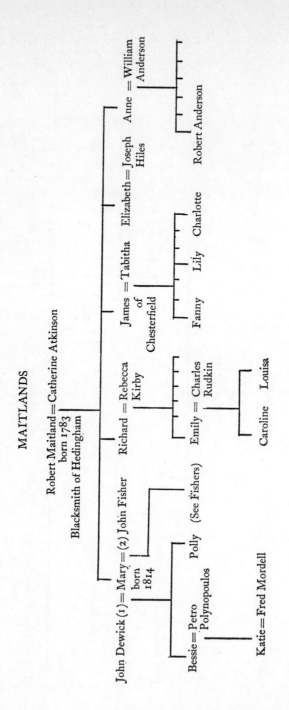

Robert Maitland = Catherine Atkinson
born 1783
Blacksmith of Hedingham

John Dewick (1) = Mary = (2) John Fisher   Richard = Rebecca   James = Tabitha   Elizabeth = Joseph   Anne = William
             born   Kirby   of   Hiles   Anderson
             1814   Chesterfield

Polly   (See Fishers)

Bessie = Petro   Emily = Charles   Fanny   Lily   Charlotte   Robert Anderson
     Polynopoulos   Rudkin

Katie = Fred Mordell   Caroline   Louisa

MILLSONS

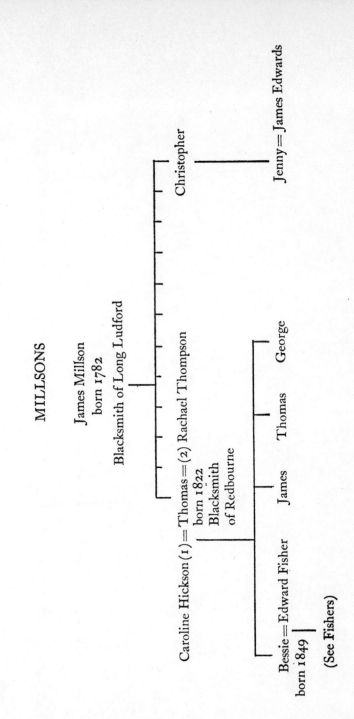

James Millson
born 1782
Blacksmith of Long Ludford

Christopher

Jenny = James Edwards

Caroline Hickson (1) = Thomas = (2) Rachael Thompson
born 1822
Blacksmith
of Redbourne

James   Thomas   George

Bessie = Edward Fisher
born 1849

(See Fishers)